FLORIDA
in
FLIGHT

JOE KNETSCH, NICK WYNNE & ROBERT J. REDD

Published by The History Press
Charleston, SC
www.historypress.com

First published 2024

Manufactured in the United States

ISBN 9781467156950

Library of Congress Control Number: 2024931858

CONTENTS

INTRODUCTION

The history of modern Florida has always been tied to the constantly evolving methods of transportation. From the early canoes and boats of Indigenous tribes to the fifteenth-century ships of European explorers and the trains and automobiles of the twentieth century, Florida grew as new transportation routes were found and exploited and as technology allowed an ever-growing population to access the multiple ports along the peninsula's coasts and the rivers and creeks that led to the interior of the jungle-like land mass. Joe Knetsch, Robert Redd and Nick Wynne—the authors of this volume—provided an overview of the importance of navigable waters to the growth of the Sunshine State in *Florida at Sea: A Maritime History* (Charleston: The History Press, 2023). *Florida in Flight: An Aviation History* is intended to do the same with a look at the evolution of manned, powered aircraft and the impact flight has had. The authors realize that the story of manned flight in Florida is a large collection of individual episodes that cannot be fully covered within the word limitations imposed by the publisher. We hope to point the way for more in-depth research by interested readers. The history of manned flight in the Sunshine State is one of excitement, a history that continues today as we reach for the heavens!

From the flimsy fabric-covered and underpowered "aeroplanes" of the early 1900s to the fast, sleek and massive passenger jets and interplanetary rockets of today to the recreational planes flown by intrepid hobbyists on weekend jaunts, aircraft have played an indisputable role in shaping what Florida is, in what it will become and in its ever-expanding economic development. The Sunshine State depends on tourism as one of the triad of critical legs of its economy—tourism, agriculture, ranching—and more than 130 million tourists arrive annually. Of that number, 35 to 50 million arrive by air at one of the state's twenty airports with regular scheduled passenger service. Without these facilities, the tourist-dependent economy, which was valued at $101.9 billion in 2021 and which supported 1.7 million workers, would be much smaller. So, too, would the numbers of annual permanent new residents, which currently is growing around 1.9 percent per year, decline. Ships, railroads and automobiles once dominated transportation to and from Florida, but those modes of transportation are declining as new aircraft arrive on the scene and newer and larger airports are developed.

In two world wars and a number of smaller conflicts, the state has been an important part of the development of military aircraft, in the training of the pilots who fly them and as a base of operations in their deployment. Many of Florida's 140 commercial airports owe their existence to their creation as training fields during World War II. In addition, the Sunshine State has seen the development in both ballistic and commercial rocketry since 1945. From the early *Bumper* series, built on captured German V-1 and V-2 technology, to manned flights to the Moon and International Space Station to the routine launches of Space X's satellites, rockets have defined modern Florida. With the development of reliable rocket vehicles, new tourist and commercial operations have emerged. So, too, have expanding technological and manufacturing ventures been opened to support them.

We invite the reader to join us as we explore the history of Florida and manned, powered flight.

THE DOMINANCE OF THE INTERNAL COMBUSTION ENGINE

Florida, in its southern part, reckons no cities of importance; it is simply studded with forts raised against the roving Indians. One solitary town, Tampa Town, was able to put in a claim in favour of its situation.
—Jules Verne, From the Earth to the Moon, *1865*

From the earliest days of the existence of humans, the idea of being able to fly has been a persistent dream. From Neolithic cave drawings to *bas-reliefs* in the Fertile Crescent, mysterious carvings in long-hidden temples in Central America, Greek and Roman mythology and religious texts found throughout the world, the idea of flying men has occupied a central role. Not just flight but controlled and powered flight. The idea was a persistent theme around the globe.

In 1783 in France, Joseph-Michel and Jacques-Étienne Montgolfier achieved recognition when they launched a tethered balloon into the skies, with Jacques-Étienne as a passenger. While a significant achievement, the balloon was not powered and, when released from its restraints, was subject to prevailing wind currents. What followed was a series of further attempts at devising some means of powering—and thereby controlling—balloons. These efforts ranged from human-powered propellers to the adaptation of heavy steam engines as a means of propulsion. In 1852, Jules Henri Giffard, a French engineer and inventor, built a small three-horsepower (2.2-kilowatt) steam engine to power a three-bladed propeller as a means of powering his 143-foot-long hot air balloon. Although he was able to travel some seventeen miles at a speed of six miles per hour, the small steam engine was too weak to overcome prevailing winds. With his limited trip, Giffard earned the distinction of being the first pilot of a powered aircraft.

Despite Giffard's success with a steam engine as a power source, further experiments with steam engines proved unworkable because of the increase in engine weight as power was increased and because of the necessity of carrying heavy water and fuel loads for use to keep the engine going. Although the early steam engines proved too heavy to power an aircraft, work on developing newer lightweight steam power plants has continued to the present day. As late as the 1960s, a California company completed drawings for a steam-powered helicopter. Although the plans were never used, the search for a viable steam power source for aircraft continues.

Still, experiments in finding alternative power sources received the most attention from inventors. In 1884, Charles Renard and Arthur C. Krebs, officers in the French Army Corps of Engineers, constructed a 165-foot-long balloon propelled by a single propeller driven by an electric motor powered by heavy batteries. On their first flight, the men made a round trip of five miles, successfully demonstrating that controlled flight was possible. The short flight also demonstrated that, like the heavier steam engines, the batteries of the day were too heavy and lacked enough power for a *sustained* flight. What was needed was a lightweight and dependable motor with long-range capabilities.

While men looked to the skies, other men were working to perfect engines that would prove to solve the problems of weight, power and reliability that could be adapted for use by aircraft. In the early 1790s, inventors and engineers in Europe and the United States began to design and experiment with internal combustion engines powered by gases or by liquid fuels. By 1823, these new engines had evolved to such a state that they had been utilized in powering vehicles and factory machines. To efficiently fuel the new engines, inventors sought a source of lightweight liquid with a highly combustible potential. The answer was petroleum—oil!

The combustible nature of petroleum was noted and used by civilizations around the world for centuries, and some progress had been made in refining crude oil, mostly collected from natural seeps, into more flammable and explosive products. Although there are some reports of oil wells as early as the ninth century, the first commercial oil well is usually credited to the efforts of Russian engineer Vasily Semyonov on a peninsula near Baku, although other individuals and locales make the same claim. The first American well was drilled by Edwin Drake in Pennsylvania in 1859.

Along with the active and ongoing efforts of explorers to find and extract new sources of petroleum, chemists kept pace by devising new refinement techniques to enhance the combustible properties of petroleum. Refined products like naphtha, kerosene and benzine soon became commercially available and were adapted for use in internal combustion engines. It was not until gasoline, which had the highest degree of combustibility, became commonplace that such engines began to be downsized while delivering higher rates of power.

As internal combustion engines became smaller and more powerful, inventors were quick to adapt them for use in horseless carriages. Although American Oliver Evans received a patent for a steam-powered amphibious carriage in 1805, it was not until 1893 that the Duryea brothers, Frank and Charles, produced the first practical American car using a one-cylinder gasoline-powered motor. Their second car, finished in 1894, demonstrated its practicality when it completed a 54-mile race at an average speed of 7.5 miles per hour. By 1895, the Duryea Motor Wagon Company was producing automobiles for sale to the public.

The success of the Duryea brothers spurred other inventors, and in 1897, the Olds Motor Vehicle Company was formed in Detroit. In 1901, Henry Ford organized a company bearing his name to manufacture automobiles, followed quickly by William Durant's General Motors Company in 1908. Although the major automobile manufacturers were located in or near Detroit, every major city and many smaller towns were home to small factories producing a variety of cars. One estimate placed the number of car companies that operated between 1893 and 1940 at more than 1,200, most of them doomed to rapid failure. The cities of Detroit, Michigan (and surrounds), and Cleveland, Ohio, eventually became the centers of automobile production, and by the 1940s, the Detroit area had become dominant—so much so that Detroit was given the sobriquet the "Motor City." By 1914, the Ford Motor Company alone was producing more than 300,000 cars for an eager American market, while the combined output for other manufacturers was less than 170,000. The next year, Ford's production numbers crossed the 500,000 mark.

Other inventors took note of the successes innovators in the automotive field had with the adoption of the internal combustion engine as a source of power and its small size, and they, too, quickly followed. As engines decreased in size and increased in power, they were attached to heavy wooden propellers on simple kite-like constructions that were piloted by daredevils, and most failed. Most, but not all.

Right: Henry Ford and the Ford Motor Company led the way in popularizing the new internal combustion engine–powered automobile in the early 1900s. *Fred Hartsook, 1919.*

Below: In 1903, the Wright brothers, Orville and Wilbur, astonished the world when they achieved the first sustained flight of a powered aircraft at Kitty Hawk, North Carolina. *National Park Service.*

On December 17, 1903, the Wright brothers, Orville and Wilbur, astonished the world with the first manned flight of a powered aircraft. From the isolated beaches of Kitty Hawk, North Carolina, the word of their achievement quickly spread around the world and touched off a global frenzy to duplicate and improve their feat. Wilbur and Orville had just become the first true airplane pilots. The first of four flights that day lasted just twelve seconds and traveled only 180 feet, but it proved that controlled human flight was possible.

The success of the Wright brothers at Kitty Hawk signaled a breakthrough in manned flight. Immediately, inventors and engineers began to think about sustained flights in substantial airframes that were safe, reliable and capable of flying miles instead of a few hundred feet. To achieve this, designers of new aircraft had to consider new concepts like "weight-to-power ratios" and revisit the laws of physics established by such early thinkers as Isaac Newton and Daniel Bernoulli that governed airflow, gravity and mass. It would take time to convert these principles into practical realities, but it would be done.

Although it would be a few years before aircraft would become a familiar sight in the Sunshine State, many civic leaders recognized the possibility that manned flights would be a staple of modern life. In 1908, city fathers in Kissimmee enacted the first ordinance to regulate flights over the city. Claiming the right to the airspace up to twenty-five miles above the town, the law forbade the flight of any "balloons, aeroplanes, heliocopters, ornithopters, or airships" within ten feet of streets and alleys or within twenty feet of any pavement in the city. The ordinance also limited the top speed of such aerial vehicles to eight miles an hour. Rebecca Maksel, writing for the *Smithsonian Magazine*'s June 2015 issue, noted that while the ordinance appeared to some to be a joke, the *Washington Post* took it seriously enough to predict, "It is safe to predict that legislation to govern the regulation of aerial traffic will before very long engage the attention of State and city legislative bodies throughout the country. And when the questions of speed, height, or proximity to congested centers of population have become the subject of animated debate it may be expected that Kissimmee, Fla., will extend the municipal chest in haughty satisfaction, for it was Kissimmee that raised a laugh some two years ago by framing a city ordinance covering the subject. The only thing that was really laughable about Kissimmee's agitation over the deviltries of aerial craft was the fact that it was somewhat premature." The ordinance also included a provision that the city council would, "[a]s soon as practicable…purchase

Lincoln Beachey, a well-known barnstormer of the pre–World War I era, is credited with making the first sustained manned flight in Florida at Orlando in 1910. *Wynne Collection.*

an aeroplane of approved modern type for the use of the marshal in the performance of his public duties, and to enable him to properly enforce the provisions of this ordinance."

Recognition for the first Florida powered flight is given to Lincoln Beachey for his demonstration flight at the Orange County Fair in Orlando in 1910. He won a $1,500 prize for staying in the air for five minutes. Two other planes competed but were not able to accomplish the feat. The likelihood is that other flights took place elsewhere in the Sunshine State, but Beachey's flight took place in a public venue before a large crowd and so received the designation "first."

Florida was a hotbed of aerial firsts during the early decades of the twentieth century. The first Florida flight school was founded in 1912. Glenn Curtiss, early aviation pioneer, established the school on Miami Beach. Soon, other flight schools were established in a number of Florida towns and cities. Several simultaneous crazes enveloped the Sunshine State as thrill seekers tested their courage on fast motorcycles, automobiles, speedboats and airplanes propelled by internal combustion engines.

With the success of the Wright brothers, other Americans rapidly took to the skies. Early planes were little more than powered gliders, and landing strips were open pasturelands or vacant golf courses. This picture accurately captures both attributes at a field near Tampa, circa 1911. *Wynne Collection.*

Although some manufacturers still persisted in producing battery-powered or steam-powered vehicles, the lack of charging stations or coaling stations for these vehicles did little to increase their popularity or to result in widespread sales.

Not everyone who wanted to learn to drive an automobile, pilot a speedboat, ride a motorcycle or soar in the heavens was motivated by adventure alone. Some individuals were quick to realize that these modern inventions could be readily adapted for commercial use. Automobiles were quickly modified for use as commercials vans; motorcycles became the mainstay for telegram and small package deliveries, fishing boats and oceangoing ships were quickly modified to accept internal combustion engines and airplanes powered by them promised faster and more flexible passenger service than trains or steamships.

In 1913, Domingo Rosillo demonstrated the possibility of transoceanic flight when he successfully completed a ninety-mile trip from Key West to Havana in his one-seat Morane-Saulnier plane. The next year, Tony Jannus, flying a two-seat Benoist, completed the first scheduled airline service when he, along with St. Petersburg mayor Abe Pheil, crossed the twenty-one-mile Tampa Bay to Tampa, thus inaugurating the St. Petersburg–Tampa Airboat Line. The initial flight took twenty-two minutes, an attractive alternative to having to spend several hours making

Pilot Tony Jannus and mechanic Albert Berry check out their Benoist flying boat prior to making the first flight of the short-lived St. Petersburg–Tampa Airboat Line. *Wynne Collection.*

the same trip by horse-drawn carriage or slow automobile. The cost of a one-way ticket was five dollars.

One month later, two navy pilots, Ensign Godfrey de Courcelles Chevalier and Lieutenant John H. Towers, inaugurated naval flight training at Pensacola when they, along with a small contingent of support

The Marine Corps established a pilot training base at Dinner Key on Biscayne Bay in Miami. Here a young lady admires a marine plane and a marine flyer. *Florida International University.*

personnel, unloaded nine disassembled planes from the USS *Mississippi*, put them together and, on February 2, 1914, took to the skies. Pensacola would become (and still remains) the center of naval aviation for the United States. The Marine Corps followed suit and, in February 1917, established its own aviation training site at the Dinner Key Naval Air Station in Miami Springs. The base, which functioned until September 1919, was closed in the aftermath of World War I, and Marine Corps training was relocated to Pensacola Naval Air Station.

Realizing that proficiency in aerial warfare had become a necessity for modern armies and based on the reports of American observers of the war in Europe, the U.S. Army decided to expand its small air force and relocate part of its number of air cadets to Florida from Texas. A suitable location for a training school was found at Arcadia, and a facility was rapidly constructed and named Carlstrom Field. Carlstrom, and the adjacent auxiliary field, Dorr Field, offered primary and advanced flight training for three hundred cadets. A second auxiliary field, Valentine Field, was also constructed at LaBelle in Lee County. Carlstrom Field operated throughout 1917 and 1918, but after the Armistice in November 1918, pilot training ceased. For about a year, the base was used to test prototypes of the "Kettering Bug," the world's first unmanned drone, which was basically a naval torpedo powered by a

Carlstrom Field and adjacent Dorr Field served as an Army Air Corps training center during World War I. The Curtiss Jenny JN-4 was the principal training plane used. In the 1930s, Carlstrom Field also served as a training base for RAF pilots. *Curtiss Aeroplane Motor Corporation.*

small internal combustion engine–driven propeller. Despite its small size, the "Bug" had a range of forty miles and traveled at a speed of seventy-five to eighty miles per hour. With the successful completion of these tests, Carlstrom Field and the base and its outlying fields were closed and the land leased to local farmers and ranchers.

The outbreak of world war had a significant impact on Florida. On the cusp of a tremendous land "boom," the war diverted the attention of Americans away from the developing explosion in Florida real estate that would quickly resume after the war. The war, however, also had a positive effect on the acceptability of the use of aircraft as a means of future travel to and around the Sunshine State. The sight of military Jennys flying through Florida skies, the stories of brave airmen in combat and the tremendous improvements made in reliability and safety of planes were common fodder for the pages of newspapers and novels. The popularity of air travel grew almost daily, a popularity that continued to grow immediately after the war when a surplus of war planes and ex-military pilots made "barnstorming" exhibitions an essential part of practically every county fair.

Like the lurking prosperity of Florida's land boom of the 1920s, so, too, was the expansion and exploitation of air travel. Although Floridians

Carlstrom Army Air Field was a major training base for army pilots during World War I. There were many crashes as inexperienced pilots took to the air. Quick-response "crash teams" on motorcycles were on hand to rescue pilots. *Florida Memory.*

would have to wait for almost a century to see the fulfillment of Jules Verne's vision of a trip to the Moon, it was enough to know that mankind could really fly—free and unfettered. The possibilities were limitless!

THE ARMY, THE MARINES, WORLD WAR I AND FLORIDA

Once you have tasted flight, you will forever walk the earth with your eyes turned skyward, for there you have been, and there you will always long to return.
—Leonardo da Vinci

The First World War came as no surprise to most Floridians. The local newspapers covered it well from the very beginning and followed the progress of the European conflict in great detail. Almost all Floridians who expressed an opinion in the local papers favored keeping out of the war and remaining neutral. Thus, the appeal of the Wilson campaign for president in 1916 for keeping the United States out of the war was favored by most Floridians. The immense slaughter of troops on all fronts was in the headlines or on the front page of nearly every newspaper and magazine available in the state. The sinking of many ships in the Atlantic and along our own coastlines shocked many, as did the *Lusitania*'s sinking and other victims of German submarines. No serious consideration was given to training our boys for combat with the notable exception of Theodore Roosevelt, Leonard Wood and others, who urged immediate preparedness. The Plattsburg experiment was not tried often elsewhere in the nation, including Florida. The thought of training flyers for the armed forces was hardly discussed in Florida or even Washington, D.C., but interest in flying was very high, as proven by Miami's expending $7,500 to hire a Wright brothers flyer to come and celebrate the city's fifteenth birthday with six demonstration flights in the summer of 1911.

Brigadier George Percival Scriven, commander of the Army Signal Corps, before World War I saw little military value in aircraft except for observation and artillery use. His attitude would change with the outbreak of war and the entry of the United States into combat. *Library of Congress.*

Part of the initial lack of interest in new inventions such as the aeroplane was because the First World War broke out just eleven years after the Wright brothers made history at Kitty Hawk. It was still a novelty at the time, and Americans were not as prepared to exploit it compared to their European counterparts. The Army Air Service, as it was called in its first years, was under the command of the Signal Corps, commanded by Brigadier General George Percival Scriven, who was skeptical of military use of the new invention for anything other than observation and reconnaissance. Indeed, in 1916, Scriven published a rather detailed report based on observations of the military attachés in each capital of the European powers' use of aircraft in combat. He even noted the use of planes in aerial bombardment. While Scriven and members of his staff understood and appreciated the development of aviation in Europe, the near total lack of technical information, closely guarded by the contending militaries, was something that would have to be overcome if the air arm of the Signal Corps was to advance.

The U.S. Army Air Corps actively recruited new pilots and mechanics during World War I with posters that differed very little from the recruiting posters used during World War II and today. *Library of Congress.*

Major problems for American airpower advocates to solve included poor funding for the tools to standardize production of planes, the lack of power in the engines then in existence in America and the lack of trained mechanics, let alone flyers, to maintain the proposed force. American pilots frequently complained about the lack of understanding by senior officers who had no experience in flying or the potential airpower represented. Most of the high-ranking officers of the army were products of the Indian Wars, some of the Spanish-American War and a few who had accompanied General Pershing's pursuit of Pancho Villa in Mexico. In this adventure, the First Aero Squadron, commanded by Captain Benjamin Foulois, experienced a number of problems that made the expedition look somewhat farcical, such as wings falling off the planes as the glue dried and cracked in the desert heat. As Edgar Raines noted, "The origins of the estrangement between the U.S. Army and its air component thus preceded the American entry into World War I."

Floridians were not ignorant of flying machines and had taken great interest in their introduction to the state. Miami was not the first city to experience a heavier-than-air machine flying over its limits. In 1910, Lincoln Beachey flew a Curtiss biplane over the city of Orlando at the first Orange County Fair. Indeed, Beachey flew every day of the fair and captured the imagination of many in the crowds. Three months later, the Curtiss team, headed by Charles Hamilton, flew over the grounds at Moncrief Park three days in succession in May 1910. Jack McCurdy flew out of Key West in early January 1911, attempting to win the prize for the first flight between Key West and Havana, Cuba. He did not make it on the first try but did succeed in getting a second plane sent to him for the return flight.

It soon became obvious to aviation pioneer Glenn Curtiss and others that Florida was ready to participate in new arial ventures. In 1911, he established one of the first flying schools in the state, even though it had to move around to find a more permanent home. Curtiss later settled in Florida permanently and contributed greatly to the development of southeastern Florida and the cities of Hialeah and Opa-locka, Florida, as well as Miami Springs. He was best known for the development of seaplanes and actually took off from the deck of a cruiser in 1910. His abilities and management skills were widely recognized in his day, and he became one of the premier trainers of navy pilots during World War I. In addition to founding a number of airfields, he also leased his land in Miami to the Marine Corps, just then getting into the action in aviation,

This is the A-1, the navy's first aircraft. It was purchased in May 1911 and was designed and built by Glenn Curtiss. *Library of Congress.*

for the sum of one dollar. During their time at the Curtiss field, the Corps trained more than two hundred officers and three hundred enlisted men stationed there. He also advised the navy to establish a naval air base on Dinner Key, which during the war earned a reputation as the most efficient naval training station in that service. Given the lovely year-round weather and relatively calm waters of Biscayne Bay, those who trained there during the war were able to fly more hours and get more training time than at any other air base. The military establishment in southeast Florida was capped off with the creation of the army's own bases at Chapman Field near Miami and Carlstrom Field near Arcadia.

The military budgets before 1916 made little mention of air power, and the continued underfunding of the aviation branches, army or navy, was a fundamental mistake in these early years of the war. Interservice rivalry played a role in this but was not the predominant cause of the underfunding. Aviation was not a priority of the Signal Corps, and the lack of concern for this was often expressed in the correspondence of the fledgling pilots. In reality, there was no true aviation industry by the time America entered the war, and this lack of corporate power meant that no one was advocating for increasing budgets.

There was little knowledge of the aerodynamics of control of flying craft and little information concerning the importance of weight and its distribution; drag and streamlining were hardly known at all. There was little initial linkage to the automotive industry for the production of motors of sufficient size and power to carry the larger and faster planes, like those being developed and flown in Europe. Prewar American designs were obsolete even before they were scheduled for production. Testing of the new designs, given the general lack of knowledge of some basic concepts, was a dangerous occupation that did cost the lives of some of the few experienced pilots available to train replacements. Once the planes went into production, there were never enough trained mechanics to maintain them and an inefficient part supply system. Management systems and distribution centers were not yet developed, and the infrastructure was primitive at best. At the beginning of the war, the United States was totally unprepared to enter at the same level of other participants. Added to these shortcomings were the constant tensions between the needs for quantity and quality in aircraft, tanks and other weapons of war, while the incessant demands for more munitions, weapons and raw materials by our new allies added pressure on the unprepared national industries.

Most of the early years of pilot training came through private vendors like the Curtiss Schools and others established in early 1917. The Curtiss School in Miami trained some of the first navy and marine pilots, and at the outbreak of war, the navy had sixty "heavier than air–rated" pilots, including those in the training status. Some had trained in the army air stations, including the first marine aviator, Alfred A. Cunningham, who received his early training at the Army Aviation School in San Diego, California, in 1916. Cunningham was a born innovator and even obtained permission to use land at the navy yard in Philadelphia to attempt to fly the "Noisy Nan," which never got off the ground. Disappointed but not discouraged, he soon joined the Aero Club of Philadelphia and soon launched his own personal campaign to get the Marine Corps interested in flying. Through his friends in Philadelphia, he was able to get the attention of Major General Commandant Biddle and soon received an appointment to Annapolis in 1912 "for duty in connection with aviation." However, no aircraft were available when he arrived, so he obtained orders to contact the Burgess Company and the Curtiss factory in Marblehead, Massachusetts, which constructed the Wright aircraft used by the navy. The instructors there gave him his first real lessons in flying, and after two hours and forty minutes of instruction, he made his first solo flight. It was not the smoothest of flights, since he had never attempted to land an airplane, but with the gas running out, he was forced to take his best shot,

McMullin School of Aviation at Drew Field, Tampa, was just one of many aviation schools that operated in Florida in the 1920s and 1930s. *Burgert Brothers Photographic Collection.*

which was successful. As quoted in *Marine Corps Aviation: The Early Years, 1912–1940*, "I got up my nerve and made a good landing, how I don't know.…This was my first solo." He was soon designated as Naval Aviator No. 5.

The second marine assigned to the aviation training at Annapolis was First Lieutenant Bernard L. "Banney" Smith, later in 1912. By the time Smith arrived, the navy had repaired its early planes, which now numbered three in total! Cunningham was assigned to fly the older of the two Wright machines, while Smith took charge of the Curtiss model. Sergeant James Maguire became the first enlisted marine to fly with Cunningham. The small group became known, informally, as the "Marine Camp." These flyers joined in with the navy flyers already commissioned into the Naval Aviation group and in 1912–13 took an active part in the experiments for detecting submarines from the air and working with air-ground communication; air-ship communication had already been experimented with using a wireless Marconi transmitter and receiver. This combination proved fairly effective in early 1913 with the exercises off Guantanamo, Cuba. They also dropped missiles from the air and took photographs of the vessels. As an added bonus, they took more than 150 marines and naval officers on "indoctrination flights." On one of these flights,

Alfred Austell Cunningham, Naval Aviator No. 5 and Marine Corp Aviator No. 1, was influential in getting the Marine Corps to start up a pilot training program and in training early Corps pilots. *Defense Visual Information Distribution Service.*

the future commandant of the Marine Corps, Lieutenant Colonel John A. Lejeune, spent fourteen hours in the air and soon became a convert to marine aviation's potential.

Naval pilot training expanded as the need grew rapidly in 1916–18. From the base in Pensacola, the navy expanded its program to Key West and Miami. The first of the Yale Units took their advanced training in West Palm Beach, but that city did not become a regular general aviation training center. Kathryn Rinehart shows that Middleburg, Florida native Captain Roy S. Geiger was the first to implement training in Miami, in April 1918. It was he who negotiated the one-dollar deal with Glenn Curtiss and began immediately training navy and marine pilots, and the old Curtiss field became the first designated Marine Flying Field. The Marine Corps even made a recruiting film, *Flying with the Marines*, which was shown nationally. The training also included "ground school, formation flying, aerobatics and tactics, gunnery and bombing, and reconnaissance" skills. There was even some practice in taking aerial photographs as a part of the training for reconnaissance. The First Marine Aviation Force was sent to Europe and played a major role in the first-ever food drop to isolated troops (a French regiment) under combat conditions. In the three months during which the unit saw combat, the unit earned thirty-two commendations, including two Medals of Honor, four Distinguished Service Medals and twenty-six Navy Crosses. It was an outstanding record for such a young squadron, but they earned every medal and honor bestowed on them. As Kathryn Rinehart noted, two of these brave marines settled in Florida following the war, and both had been trained in Miami.

On paper, the establishment of bases and supplies appears simple, but in fact it was a difficult affair. Some of the training planes, like the B-1, were particularly noted in the correspondence. The B-1 flown by Cunningham was a concoction built of old, sometimes spare, parts that did not fit exactly. With many makers of motors and parts, little standardization took place, making repairs very questionable. As noted by Cunningham in his report to

Lieutenant T. Ellyson and an unidentified mechanic test the Curtiss flying boat, which became the navy's first fully operational aircraft. *Library of Congress.*

Harry Land of Bradenton, a pilot in the 84th Aero Squadron, poses in the cockpit of his "Hat in the Ring" airplane. *Manatee County Public Library.*

Captain Chambers: "My machine, as I told you and Mr. Towers probably told you, is not, in my opinion, fit for use. I built it from parts of the Burgess F and Wright B, which are not exactly alike and nothing fitted. I had to cut off and patch up parts and bore additional holes in beams in order to make them fit." This is hardly a recommendation to use his machine, and he even noted that Lieutenant "Hap" Arnold of the army, later commander of the Army Air Corps during World War II, thought that the machine was so dangerous he doubted if any army pilot would fly it. Cunningham was an intrepid flyer, and despite its many faults, he took the B-1 on more than four hundred flights between October 1912 and July 1913. At best, he reached the flying time of about eighty miles and reached an altitude of around eight hundred feet. However, his flight logs tell us of the more difficult days between flights number 371 and 383, where the logs simply state, "Engine stopped in air on nearly all these flights." In August 1913, Cunningham requested a detachment from flight duty. The reason given: his fiancée refused to marry him unless he gave up flying. No one can blame her for that view, and he did indeed get a transfer to the Washington Navy Yard, where he continued to advocate for naval/marine aviation.

Lieutenant John H. Towers inaugurated naval flight training at Pensacola when he, along with a small contingent of support personnel, unloaded nine disassembled planes from the USS *Mississippi*, put them together and, on February 2, 1914, took to the skies. *Library of Congress.*

Lieutenants T. Ellyson and John H. Towers at the controls of the A-2, the second plane in the navy's inventory. *Library of Congress.*

The navy had its problems with the bureaus, as did the army, but the latter had the advantage of being "in the business" longer. Captain Benjamin Foulois had been one of the first flyers for the army, having accompanied Wilbur Wright as an observer during the testing of the Wrights' planes for use by the army. In 1916, he helped to form the First Aero Squadron, which went along with the forces of General John J. Pershing across the border with Mexico in search of Pancho Villa and his men. The squadron began with eight aircraft, none of which actually survived the expedition, but they did provide some valuable reconnaissance for the troops, especially the lay of the land. The mechanical failures of the Jennys and other craft on this expedition led to widespread skepticism as to the value of investing in the airplanes. However, one of the early converts to the potential military use of airplanes was the commander of the expedition, General John J. Pershing. The general did not put the blame on the flyers or the mechanics assigned to the unit, but much of the blame went on the manufacturers of the craft.

Many things about designing and building airplanes were unknown at this time, like the aerodynamics of flight, the role of weight in the handling of the craft, the engine power needed to sustain flight for long distances, what substances could be properly used to construct the aircraft and much more. Did we have the right kind of wood (when frames were made of it); was the canvas that covered the body of the plane available, especially since the main manufacturers of canvas were predominantly in Ireland, now cordoned off by the German submarines; and what did we lack in technology compared with the allies/enemies? Every belligerent in the war had better and more advanced airplanes than did the unprepared United States.

What delayed the United States from developing its air arm was, in part, the interservice rivalries, the bureaucratic intransigents and the policies of the Wilson administration that "had kept us out of war." The lack of funding from Congress and the lack of imagination by the old vets of the army, none of whom had a clear idea of modern warfare, was a recipe for disaster. Not even the dogged pushing for funding by Foulois and the pressure from rising young officers like William "Billy" Mitchell was enough to overcome the lack of support from these. Of course, there were individuals who soon took the lead and forced the issue. Foremost among the proponents of adding air power to the American arsenal was General Pershing and his younger staff members, many of whom would make their marks in the next war. The Army Air Service, created in 1918, was, like the Signal Corps, a separate branch of service under the aegis of the army. But the army was not totally immune to the pressure of proponents for modernization, and many innovations soon began to appear, one of which was the purchase or leasing of properties for training members of the new Army Air Service.

Sites were needed to train this new arm of the military, even if it was confined or assigned to the Signal Corps. The Signal Corps was not opposed to the air component of its new command, but it was skeptical. The 1916 study by Brigadier General George P. Scriven, the chief Signal Corps officer, became the basis for another, more influential study by the staff of the War College that was published in pamphlet form and in the *Field Artillery Journal*. As Edgar Raines has noted, "More descriptive than analytical, it nevertheless noted the introduction of specialized 'bombing aircraft' which picked up momentum during the war but even more so after it." In late 1915, the Signal Corps was planning on equipping enough planes to provide each army division with a squadron of eight observation planes for battlefield observation and artillery spotting. Additionally, each squadron was to have two "high speed machines" with the ability to defend the observation units

The 1927 movie *Wings*, which featured Clara Bow and Charles "Buddy" Rogers, popularized the newly formed Army Air Service for Americans. The movie also featured a young Gary Cooper in a supporting role. *Paramount Pictures.*

The Army Signal Corps released the first specifications for competitive bids for a two-seater observation plane in 1908. The Wright military flyer, a twin-propeller open-cockpit plane, was adopted and entered service in 1909. This was the first aircraft operated by the U.S. military. *Library of Congress.*

and provide long-range reconnaissance and an additional two planes for bombardment missions.

By European standards, the Army Air Service was small and technically backward without any coherent doctrine on which to operate. Being the late entry into the war, the United States had to adopt and adapt quickly and with large numbers if it was to have a voice in the final peace arrangements. Lacking time to develop their own doctrine and methods of employing the air service, General Pershing wisely adopted the systems already developed after three years of war by the French and English Air Corps. This covered balloons, reconnaissance planes, fighter escorts and large-scale bombing missions.

The information gathered at the training schools of Europe was quickly adopted by the United States. Since the Army Air Service could offer few serviceable airplanes, almost every plane flown by an American pilot in Europe was made in either France, England or Italy. Training to familiarize American pilots with the Spads, Nieuports and Sopwith Camels was done by French instructors who spoke little English. The final manning, training and equipping of squadrons took place in France at organization and training centers. Pilots, aircraft, vehicles, tools and a large assortment of other equipment and details were assembled at these centers to prepare these formations for combat.

The Allies needed American manpower and spirit to meet the German onslaught, especially in early 1918. The Allies, therefore, were willing to share a great deal of technical details and expertise. Much of this material exchange came as the result of the "Bolling Mission" to France, which initiated the purchase of European air equipment and planes. France, which supplied nearly 80 percent of the planes flown by Americans during the war, was eager to provide the expertise to get the Americans up to or near the level of French, British and Italian flyers. The August 30, 1917 agreement called for the French to provide 875 training aircraft and 5,000 service-type airplanes. If they could not meet this very high demand, the Americans would be free to buy from England and Italy. The leader of the commission, Raynal Bolling, did his job so well that Pershing asked him to stay in France and help with the transition of the air service from the Signal Corps to the regular army.

In the United States, the result of the Bolling Mission was to highlight the need to create training facilities for the new Army Air Service. The army sent out teams of engineers and construction personnel to examine a number of sites. Arizona ranked number one in the selection process because of its long periods of sunshine and flying weather. Florida ranked second in potential because of its relatively flat geography, excellent weather and available space. This resulted in the leasing of the lands that became Carlstrom and Dorr Fields, located in rural DeSoto County near the city of Arcadia. Carlstrom was about six miles southeast of the

The French Nieuport fighter was one of the foreign-made aircraft flown by American pilots in battle during World War II. *Royal Air Force Museum.*

then limits of the city, and building began in January 1918. The field covered nearly seven hundred acres, which eventually included fourteen hangars; six barracks, which housed 175 men each; and a hospital. Dozens of smaller buildings housed the headquarters group, maintenance and officers' quarters. Initially, the men lived in tents, which were frequently visited by the "state bird" of Florida: the mosquito. The food was not particularly good, surely not the "gourmet" dinners American mothers often fixed.

Letters from trainees indicate exactly the type of training given at Carlstrom and its companion post, Dorr Field. Both of these airfields were for advanced training, which is why most of the cadets were transferred from other bases, most frequently Rich Field in Waco, Texas, which provided the basic flying skills needed to get the planes aloft and steady. The main squadrons trained and noted at Carlstrom were the 76th and the 107th, 108th and 109th. The main coursework was for those in these "pursuit squadrons," used as escorts for observation teams or bombers. It was an intense six-week course using the JN-4 Jennys as the standard aircraft and broken down into several phases. The first phase stressed acrobatics, which included difficult, evasive maneuvers including the "vertical reverse," a move that saved many airmen over the course of the war. After that phase was completed, the trainees moved on to learning the ins and outs of scout patrol formations. After this had been completed, the squadron would be transferred to Dorr Field, where aerial gunnery was taught.

Dorr Field, located about thirteen miles southwest of Arcadia, was very similar in construction to Carlstrom. It contained forty-six buildings when completed and had fourteen hangars, six barracks and its own hospital. It was opened on March 15, 1918, just two months after Carlstrom. It, too, was an advanced training facility with a specialty of gunnery. Its graduates scored a large number of combat victories in Europe, which gave the people of DeSoto County a feeling that the government would keep it open after the war was over. It did stay open until November 1919, when all training stopped and the remaining units transferred out. The sharply reduced budgets of the years following the war precluded any further development of the base. Like its companion base, it was then put into a dormant state. It did share some training of primary pilots for a few short years, but the army could not justify the number of such facilities in such widely dispersed areas as Texas, California and Florida.

Throughout the 1920s and 1930s, most of the land at Dorr Field was leased out to local farmers. However, as soon as the war cloud began to gather

A crashed Curtiss JN-4 at Carlstrom Army Air Field in 1918. Such crashes were not unusual, although some could be deadly. *Florida Memory.*

in Europe again, Dorr and Carlstrom were reopened for flight training in October 1941, just a month and a half before the attack on Pearl Harbor.

The only other army flying base used for training in Florida during the war was Chapman Field, known for its gunnery school, and the Cutler Aerial Gunnery Field, known for its intense training of pilots and observers in the use of machine guns. Of the three bases, it was the most modern military facility in Florida. Its position on the Cutler Ridge meant that to get water and electricity to the buildings, some serious digging through the limestone base was essential. The water storage tank for the base had a capacity of 100,000 gallons, which provided some of the drinking water and operation for the hydrant system for firefighting. It was a model community with its own sewerage system, a hospital with operating room and an entertainment center operated by the Knights of Columbus and the local YMCA. Many of the roads to and from the base are still used today in Dade County. On November 15, 1918, the name of the field was officially changed to the Victor Chapman Military Reservation by Major Kenly, then head of the Aeronautical Division. Victor Chapman was the first flyer killed in action in France during the war. The war ended officially three days after the renaming ceremony, but construction continued until the work was

Right: Glenn Curtiss, an early American aviation pioneer, actively promoted military training bases in Florida, including the army base at Chapman Field and the Marine Corps base at Dinner Key. Both were close to Miami. *Wikimedia Commons.*

Below: Although of poor quality, this photograph captures the members of the Escadrille Americaine, who flew combat in World War I. On the extreme left is Victor E. Chapman, the first American airman killed in the war. Other members of the squadron are identified on the photograph. *Earlyaviators.com.*

The first class of naval aviators at Pensacola Naval Air Station poses for a class picture in 1914. *Florida Memory.*

completed in March 1919. A contract was a contract, and the army lived up to that concept at that time.

Chapman Field was transferred to several entities in the postwar decades, eventually becoming part of the University of Miami and the U.S. Department of Agriculture's Subtropical Horticulture Research facility.

The First World War brought Florida into the front lines of preparing American fighting men (and women) for the contest. The lessons learned were many. When the next war came, they would be put to use when the state became a major training area for the major military services and the Coast Guard. The Pensacola Naval Air Station is still important today, and the creation of many of the bases in and around Hillsborough and Pinellas Counties during World War II have their origins in the lessons from World War I. The old army philosopher Emory Upton noted long ago the constant tendency in democracies like ours to get back to "normalcy" and to reduce military spending after every major conflict. This pattern has cost us dearly in the past.

BARNSTORMING, AIR RACES AND DELIVERING THE MAIL

They're all frightfully keen,
those magnificent men in their flying machines.
They can fly upside with their feet in the air,
They don't think of danger, they really don't care.
Newton would think he had made a mistake,
To see those young men and the chances they take.
—Those Magnificent Men in Their Flying Machines *(1965)*

As early as 1909, Charles Foster Willard, who learned to fly under the tutelage of Glenn Curtiss and became airplane pilot number four, took his Curtiss-built "Golden Flyer" on exhibition flights around the United States. In 1910, he became a nationally recognized flyer when he completed a fifty-five-mile trip over Los Angeles in a biplane powered by a fifty-horsepower gasoline engine. Because of his numerous appearances promoting airplanes, he earned the title of the "First Barnstormer." On some of his visits to various states, Willard became the first aviator to gain recognition as the pilot of the first officially recorded flight in that state. Charles F. Willard also gained notoriety when he became the first person to be shot down in an airplane when an irate farmer took a shot at his plane and hit his propeller. An engineer by profession, Willard enjoyed a long career as a designer of aircraft, including flying boats for Glenn Curtiss. Born in 1883, he died in 1977 after a long career in aviation.

A Curtiss C-2 flying boat takes off from the deck of the USS *North Carolina* in Pensacola Bay in 1915. *Smithsonian Institution.*

A rescue boat stands by during the 1915 launch of a Curtiss C-2 flying boat from the deck of the USS *North Carolina*. *Smithsonian Institution.*

The years before the Great War saw numerous demonstration flights of varying distances and speed made across the nation, but it was not until after the war that barnstorming events became more than a mere novelty. World War I brought myriad changes to the United States and to the world in general. Perhaps none was as important as the acceptance of mobile machines and the almost universal reliance on the internal combustion engine, powered by gasoline and capable of being sized up or down to fit a particular job. Despite the fame of aviators worldwide and the glamour associated with flying, the number of planes actually available in the early 1920s was limited. The single greatest source of aircraft was the U.S. Army decision to downsize its air arm and sell thousands of Jennys, the basic training and combat plane manufactured by Glenn Curtiss. Soon the skies over local and state fairs, community gatherings or virtually every makeshift airport hosted one of the many traveling barnstormer shows that featured daredevil stunts and aerobatic performances. Soon, too, average Americans were offered the opportunity to "touch the face of God" for as little as five dollars for a fifteen-minute ride. Although the overall safety record of airplanes was good, there was still the element of danger of engine failure or some other accidental happening. Despite the dangers, there were willing customers who paid to become passengers.

Simply offering short rides was not enough to sustain barnstorming as a business venture, so pilots added a variety of dangerous stunts to entice paying customers to watch their shows. Wingwalkers, plane-to-plane in-flight transfers, automobile-to-plane stunts, simulated air combat, aerobatics, parachute jumps and a host of other dangerous tricks made up the programs of these itinerant exhibitions. Although some barnstormers flew separately and operated independently, some entrepreneurs realized that a single flyer in a single plane soon exhausted the patience and interest of paying viewers, while a group of flyers, each with his or her own specialty, could keep the action going long enough to satisfy the most critical of fans. Mechanical failures, crashes or other problems that might cancel a show with a single plane were overcome by several planes and multiple pilots. Soon flying exhibitions offered attendees spectacles that featured extended performances by many individuals and groups. Like their predecessors in the world of mass entertainment, these "circuses" provided a steady stream of act after act, some occurring simultaneously.

The names of these death-defying men and women, for there was no prohibition against women participating nor were there many racial restrictions, were as well known to most Americans as collegiate and

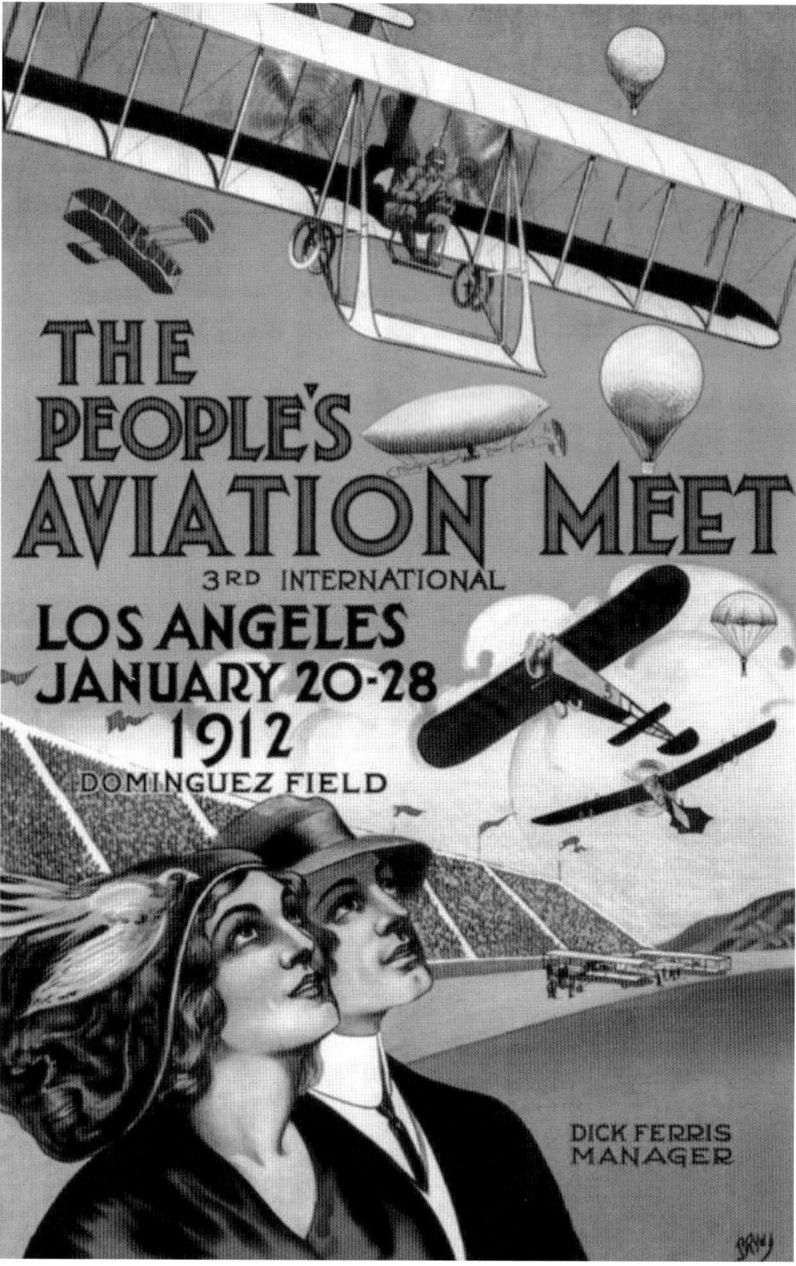

Air shows, sometimes called "meets," were effective ways to introduce the public to the world of flying in the first three decades of the twentieth century. Shows featured acrobatic performers, aerobatics and a variety of aircraft. Some shows also offered rides in airplanes for a nominal fee. *Los Angeles County Museum of Art.*

professional football and baseball players are today. Mabel Cody and Her Flying Circus, Tex Johnston, Wiley Post, Bessie Coleman, Harriet Quimby, Charles Lindbergh, Roland Garros, Tony Jannus and Roscoe Turner were just a few of the hundreds of barnstormers in the United States. So great was the international fame of some of these flyers that they found ready audiences in Europe, South America and around the globe.

Each nation produced its own barnstormers, some of whom would later rise to positions of importance in commercial and military aviation. For example, Ernst Udet, the second-highest-scoring German World War I ace (sixty-two kills), maintained his fan base by barnstorming after the war. His fame would ultimately see him placed in command of Luftwaffe aircraft development in the late 1930s. The failure of the Luftwaffe in the Battle of Britain, for which he was blamed, however, resulted in his suicide. Louis Blériot, a manufacturer of automobile headlights in the early 1900s, used the profits from his company to fund experiments in aviation. During the first decades of the 1900s, he built experimental planes and flew them in demonstrations throughout France. Following World War I, his company became the leader of aircraft manufacturing in France.

Not all barnstormers performed over small airfields or fairgrounds solely. Some set their sights much higher. Amelia Earhart, for example, combined her barnstorming appearances with attempts at setting world records for distance and speed. So, too, did Bessie Coleman, Charles Lindbergh and Jimmy Doolittle. The U.S. military participated in many of the events by sponsoring pilots and airplanes in events aimed at setting new records.

Despite the persistent popularity of barnstorming performances, they had begun to die out by the mid-1920s. The imposition of safety regulations for performers, the requirements for pilot and aircraft certification and the development of faster and more sophisticated planes lessened the appeal of outdated World War I planes. Gradually, the supply of the venerable open-cockpit Jennys and Spads diminished, replaced by sleek, metal-encased monoplanes with powerful new engines that cost thousands of dollars. Gradually, too, barnstorming events changed to highly organized races around established tracks or endurance races that covered hundreds and thousands of miles. The visits of itinerant pilots to local events became a thing of the past as flying lost its novelty and became more commonplace.

As aircraft technology advanced, records fell on a regular basis as new planes became available. Perhaps the most notable of all these records was that established by Charles Lindbergh when he crossed the Atlantic Ocean alone in his *Spirit of St. Louis*, a single-engine monoplane, in May 1927.

The Jannus brothers flew regularly scheduled routes from St. Petersburg to Tampa and back for three consecutive months in 1914. *Wynne Collection.*

Lindbergh's accomplishment focused attention once again on barnstorming, and the premiere of Paramount's World War I epic movie *Wings* added to the renewed frenzy over flyers and flying. The leather jackets and caps, high boots and jodhpurs that constituted the basic dress for aviators became fashion statements for the "in" crowd, and every young lad and lassie wanted to own their own leather caps, complete with goggles.

In 1937, aviatrix Amelia Earhart and navigator Fred Noonan claimed the attention of the world as they embarked from Miami on an around-the-world flight in a two-engine Lockheed Electra. Although the two were tragically lost over the Pacific Ocean, their journey was covered in detail by virtually every newspaper and radio station in the world, and the mystery of what happened to them remains a popular subject of conspiracists and aviation historians.

Famed aviatrix Amelia Earhart poses with her new convertible in front of a Lockheed Electra, the airplane she would pilot on her ill-fated 'round-the-world trip with navigator Fred Noonan. *Smithsonian Institution.*

Not only did the exploits of barnstormers provide entertainment for the general public, but they also achieved other things. First, despite the occasional plane crashes or deaths of aerial performers, the overall safety record of flying was good enough to attract entrepreneurs who saw the possibilities of commercial air travel as a profitable business. Although the Jannus brothers had demonstrated the feasibility of regularly scheduled passenger service with their cross–Tampa Bay, St. Petersburg–Tampa airline in 1914, flying was still in its infancy, and neither the number of available planes nor their passenger capacity was sufficient to sustain the operation of such a service. The airline lasted for only four months.

By the mid-1920s, however, the situation was changing. Several technological factors were important. First, newer and larger aircraft were designed and manufactured by a multitude of companies formed for that purpose. These newer aircraft abandoned the wood and canvas designs of the first two decades of the 1900s and used aluminum frames

On January 1, 1914, Tony Jannus inaugurated scheduled air service when he flew from St. Petersburg to Tampa with St. Petersburg's mayor, Abe Pheil, as a passenger. *Wynne Collection.*

and skins instead. Not only were the new planes sturdier and safer than their predecessors, but they were also larger and could accommodate more passengers and cargo. At the same time, gasoline engines were also increasing in size and horsepower. When mated with the new airframes, particularly in multi-engine configurations, the result was aircraft that were faster and could travel longer distances. With these innovations, however, came minor problems such as excessive noise and vibration. Still, the number of airline passengers continued to grow each year despite these problems.

In the 1920s and 1930s, it was possible to fly, mostly, from the East Coast of the United States to the Pacific coast, but it was expensive and took several days. At an average cost of $260, about half the cost of a new Ford automobile, flying was usually reserved for the rich or for businessmen. Because flights were usually restricted to daylight hours, long-distance flights were made in stages, with passengers transferred to trains to continue their journey at night. A transcontinental flight across the United States took three or four days and involved several transfers. Until technology could solve the problems inherent in night flying, travel by air would remain a unique and adventuresome experience.

Two inventions, still in their infancy, offered solutions to the limitations of night flying. The first was the use of radio communications between aircraft and ground stations. Invented by Guglielmo Marconi in 1895, wireless radio was initially limited to transmitting Morse code, but in 1906 Reginald Fessenden invented a way to make voice transmissions. Although it was unreliable and limited in range, he and other inventors continued to work to improve its efficiency. By the end of World War I, crude radio systems using Morse code had been installed in some airplanes for use by artillery spotters. Although not much appreciated by pilots who used this rudimentary system, the system proved that ground-to-air direct communications were possible. Radio technology continued to evolve to the point that it became viable commercially, and KDKA, the first commercial radio station, debuted on November 2, 1920, in Pittsburgh, Pennsylvania. Soon virtually every American home had a radio, and commercial radio stations were operating in all major cities and large towns.

As radio transmitters and receivers became more effective, they were soon added to aircraft. Experiments by the U.S. Army Air Corps, the Ford Motor Company and various individuals resulted in the creation of new navigation aids, principally low-frequency radio beams, that allowed pilots to safely fly at night and during inclement weather. By the end of the 1920s, pilots whose planes were equipped with the new systems were able to complete their flights in total darkness, heavy rainstorms and snowstorms by following radio beams transmitted by strategically located stations. The high cost of such systems, however, limited their initial usage. By the mid-1930s, however,

A large crowd gathered to witness the first flight of the new airline between St. Petersburg and Tampa on January 1, 1914. *Wynne Collection.*

Leo Rosenberg broadcasting the Harding-Cox presidential election returns on KDKA. Pictured are R.S. McClelland, William Thomas, Rosenberg and John Frazier. The event represented the nation's first commercial radio broadcast. *Senator John Heinz History Center.*

more and more commercial airlines added the systems and absorbed the costs as a business necessity.

In 1928, experiments by the Army Air Corps demonstrated the viability of flying "blind," using only instruments. James H. Doolittle, an internationally known competitive pilot and flight instructor, navigated a plane from takeoff to landing using only artificial horizontal and directional gyroscopes developed by Lawrence Sperry as guides. Although another pilot who could see accompanied him on the flight, Doolittle, who was sealed in a separate compartment with no visibility, successfully completed the feat. Sperry and others continued to develop better instruments for this purpose. In addition to his work on instruments for "blind" flying, Sperry also continued to upgrade an earlier invention of his: the automatic pilot. This instrument when engaged maintained the equilibrium of aircraft in flight and also maintained the speed and course determined by the pilot. Once again, this expensive system was gradually added to the fleets of commercial aircraft and adopted by the military for use in warplanes.

Despite the continuing advances in aircraft technology and its adoption by commercial carriers, there were simply not enough paying customers in

The U.S. Post Office, which subsidized airmail flights, urged the public to utilize this service in order to generate funds to pay for the subsidies. *Smithsonian Institution.*

the 1920s and 1930s to sustain a profitable airline. The U.S. Post Office provided a solution—just as it had done with steamboats, trains and the Pony Express—by offering subsidies for mail deliveries. In 1918, the Postal Service experimented with airmail deliveries when it established a major air route between Washington, D.C., and New York City. Although the initial payments for this service were based on the weight of the mail carried, it did provide additional payments for equipment upgrades and navigation aids. Gradually, additional feeder routes were added to the original route that expanded the area covered greatly.

In 1925, Congress passed the so-called Kelly Act (Air Mail Act), which mandated the transfer of airmail routes to private companies. By this action, Congress intended to provide a source of steady income for emerging airlines and give them time to develop an expanded customer base. In 1926, Congress expanded its assistance to emerging airlines through the passage of the Air Commerce Act, which saw the establishment of a new branch of the Commerce Department called the Aeronautics Branch, which was the forerunner of the Federal Aviation Administration. The new Aeronautics Branch quickly established procedures for licensing pilots and for the certification of all aircraft as to their safety and air worthiness. In addition, the branch provided financial assistance in establishing new navigation aids along major air routes.

The new system of subsidizing airmail companies was successful, but because the bulk of airmail flown was relatively small, most of these companies utilized small planes with limited space, which were more efficient to operate. As a result, the development of passenger-oriented airlines was slow and limited to routes between major cities. In 1930, Congress addressed this issue by passing the McNary-Watres Act, which amended the Air Mail Act of 1925. The new legislation made more money available for subsidies, changed air routes, based subsidy payments on aircraft size and available space and encouraged smaller airmail companies to merge with passenger airlines. Postmaster General Walter Folger Brown, a firm believer in the

Left: Melville Clyde Kelly, a member of the House of Representatives from Pennsylvania, introduced a resolution to permit private contracting of airmail service, the Air Mail Act of 1925, which subsidized the operations of airlines. *Library of Congress.*

Right: Postmaster Walter Folger Brown, in office from 1929 until 1933, sparked a Congressional investigation into his practice of awarding airmail contracts that favored larger airlines. *Library of Congress.*

future of air travel, took an active role in promoting closer ties between small airmail companies and larger airlines. In a May 1930 meeting with airline executives to implement the McNary-Watres Act, he assumed control of the proceedings when no consensus could be reached and assigned air routes and service territories himself without the agreement of the executives.

Fallout from Brown's action came quickly. Dubbing the meeting with Brown as the "Spoils Conference," several small airmail companies used their economic clout to persuade members of Congress to hold hearings on Brown's actions. Amid charges of conspiracy, corruption and favoritism, President Franklin D. Roosevelt sought to defuse the so-called crisis by canceling all domestic contracts with the post office and assigning the task of delivering the mail to the Army Air Corps. In February 1934, the air corps assumed the task, but after a series of accidents and several deaths from crashes and loud public outrage at the "senseless deaths" of popular flyers like Eddie Rickenbacker and Charles A. Lindbergh, Congress passed the Air Mail Act of 1934, which relieved the air corps of this job and brought order and stability to the industry and an end to the crisis. Subsidy payments were reduced, some smaller airline received contracts, aviation holding companies were dissolved, airlines were separated as corporate entities from airplane manufacturers and previous holders of mail contracts were forced to change their names and their corporate structures. In the process, several well-known and powerful airline executives—accused of corruption—were fired and barred from the airlines industry. In addition, authority for supervising and awarding of new contracts was split between the Commerce Department, the Post Office Department and the Interstate Commerce Commission. With the implementation of the Air Mail Act of 1934, the separation between airmail companies and passenger airlines was gradually erased.

During the wrangling over which company would be granted contracts to carry the mail, the new administration of Franklin D. Roosevelt was undertaking other measures to assist the airline industry as a whole. In November 1933, FDR unveiled one of his earliest New Deal "make work" projects, the Civil Works Agency (CWA), which provided millions of jobs for unskilled workers during the harsh winter of 1933–34 as part of the larger Federal Emergency Relief Administration (FERA). Although short-lived (the program ended in March 1934), the CWA provided temporary jobs for some 4 million persons who were used to create or improve basic infrastructure assets for communities—roads, schools, sewers and municipal airports. During its short life, the CWA built or expanded one thousand airports, replacing crude dirt runways and pastures with paved ones that could handle the larger planes that were being manufactured. The new airports greatly expanded the number of possible destinations for the rapidly growing domestic and international airline industries. The use of federal programs to fund such programs would continue throughout the 1930s as the Public Works Administration and the Works Progress Administration were implemented as part of the New Deal.

Despite the ongoing Depression, which slowed the nation's economy, the McNary-Watres Act boosted the use of airlines for travel, and the industry experienced a decade of growth. Gradually, airline travel, which had once been affordable only for the rich, became more prevalent as ticket prices were reduced to an affordable level for the middle class. The controversy surrounding the delivery of the mail and passenger airlines produced positive changes in the industry. The passage of the various Air Mail Acts to resolve disputes demonstrated that the federal government recognized the value of establishing safe, reliable and expanding uses of aircraft in furthering public services and that the federal government was willing to use its budgetary power to promote the continuing expansion of the industry. The passage of the acts also demonstrated that the same government that was willing to subsidize the aircraft/airline industries was not averse to using its regulatory authority to ensure that this growth and the attendant safety issues proceeded in an orderly and safe manner. These are powers that the federal government continues to expand and strengthen today.

FLORIDA THE MAGNIFICENT

Florida is unique; its climate, its soil and the products of the soil, its geography and topography, its birds, beasts, and fishes, its trees and flowers, are outside of the experience of the people of the rest of the United States.
—Florida in the Making, *January 1, 1926*

So wrote Frank Parker Stockbridge and John Holliday Perry in their popular tome praising the attributes of the Sunshine State at the very height of the Florida Boom of the first half of the decade of the 1920s. Despite their detailed descriptions of its physical features and its transportation networks, the authors made no mention of the state's emerging air-related activities. Indeed, when discussing transportation networks and the extensive coverage of water, rail and automobile routes, the prospect of air travel as a key to the future development of the Sunshine State was completely ignored. In reality, however, civic and commercial leaders throughout the state were watching what was going on in Congress with the passage of the Kelly Act of 1925 and the creation of a national airmail service, and they realized the importance of being included in the system. In many Florida towns, open pastureland and golf courses were quickly converted into crude landing strips that could accommodate the small planes carrying mail. Some cities—such as Tampa, Jacksonville and Miami—had multiple airports located in large suburbs or adjacent towns. In Miami, for example, there were five airports, excluding the Marine Training Field at Dinner Key.

One of the earliest airlines to operate in the Sunshine State was Aeromarine Airways, which began operations in November 1920 with an inaugural flight between Key West and Havana, Cuba. Using flying boats manufactured by the Aeromarine Plane and Motor Company, its parent company, the airline transported passengers, freight and mail to and from Cuba and the Bahamas. Soon, however, Aeromarine Airways expanded its service routes to include major towns in Florida, as well as New York, Chicago and Atlantic City. Unfortunately, the airline, like many of its competitors, depended on airmail contracts to subsidize its passenger operations, and when the U.S. Post Office imposed a temporary freeze on such contracts in 1924, Aeromarine Airways ceased operations. During its short existence, however, the company claimed a number of airline firsts: the first U.S. international airmail service and first scheduled U.S. international passenger service; the first total-service U.S. airline in existence that carried mail, freight and passengers on the same flight; and the first in-flight movie when passengers were treated to the movie *Howdy, Chicago* as the plane circled the city. All of the innovations were not enough to save the airline, and it failed.

One year after the demise of Aeromarine Airways, Congress passed the Kelly Act in 1925, which mandated that airmail delivery was to be carried out by private companies. Routes between population centers were quickly established, contracts let, pilots hired and operations started, and where mail planes landed, passenger service quickly followed. The first airline to be awarded a mail contract in Florida was Florida Airways, which was founded by World War I hero Eddie Rickenbacker in 1923 and based in Jacksonville at Paxon Field. Although it had secured a mail contract, the revenue from that was not enough to support airline operations. According to aviation historian David T. Courtwright, wet letters and bricks were airmailed back and forth between the cities because subsidies were paid based on the weight of cargoes, and this was a simple way to increase the weight and raise incoming revenue. In 1926, Florida Airways introduced passenger service between Miami and Jacksonville, but the high price of sixty dollars for a one-way ticket limited the number of flyers. Although the airline flew the all-metal Stout 2-AT, known as the Air Pullman and which could accommodate nine passengers at a time, that year only 939 paying customers took advantage of this faster way to travel. Although Florida Airways attempted to shore up its finances by offering air travel to Cuba, this effort failed because Juan Trippe and Pan American Airways had secured the exclusive landing rights for that country. Florida Airways closed its doors in June 1927.

One of the earliest airlines to operate in the Sunshine State was the Aeromarine Airways, which began operations in November 1920 with an inaugural flight between Key West and Havana, Cuba. *Smithsonian Institution.*

Aeromarine Airways soon expanded its routes to major Florida cities and to Chicago, New York and Atlantic City. This photograph shows the seaplane *Niña* docked in Tampa's Hillsborough Bay in 1922. *Burgert Brothers Photographic Collection.*

Florida Airways, under the leadership of World War I ace Eddie Rickenbacker, was the first Florida airline to receive an airmail contract under the Air Mail Act of 1925. *Smithsonian Institution.*

SOME 1920S AND 1930S FLORIDA MUNICIPAL AIRPORTS

City	*Date Founded*
St. Augustine	1916
Inverness Landing Field	1920s
Fort Myers	1926
Titusville	1927
Melbourne	1928
DeLand	1920s
St. Petersburg	1929
Winter Haven	1925
Fort Lauderdale	1929
Jacksonville (Paxon Field)	1920
Jacksonville (Municipal)	1927
Orlando	1928
Venice	1936
Tampa (Drew Field)	1926
Tampa (Davis Island)	1935

Eddie Rickenbacker, with pilot Paul Foster, by the door of an Eastern Airlines Lockheed Electra 10, July 25, 1935. *Auburn University Special Collections.*

The failure of Florida Airways did not lessen the appeal of airmail contracts or a potentially expanding passenger base, and two months after this failure, Harold Pitcairn, the founder of Pitcairn Aviation, was awarded the routes of the failed airline. Pitcairn expanded the number of cities served and added freight service, along with limited passenger service. Where Florida Airways had failed, Pitcairn Aviation thrived and eventually morphed into Eastern Airlines. The passenger planes owned by Florida Airways were sold to Stout Air Services, which was the forerunner of United Airlines. Despite the failure of Florida Airways, the dream of providing reliable and affordable air service persisted.

Pitcairn Aviation, founded by aircraft manufacturer Harold Pitcairn from the bankrupt Florida Airways, provided both airmail delivery and passenger service. Pitcairn Aviation eventually became Eastern Airlines. *Smithsonian Institution.*

In 1927, three former Army Air Corps pilots—Carl Spaatz, Henry "Hap" Arnold and John Jouett—concerned about the growing influence and operations of German-backed airlines in Central and South America, created Pan American Airways as a way to counteract what they perceived as foreign infringement in an American sphere of influence. Although Pan American was placed under the supervision of a civilian, Juan Trippe, after merging with two other companies to form the Aviation Corporation of the Americas, its creation marked the first time that air power was considered to be an effective geopolitical tool of the federal government. Using Sikorsky S-40 flying boats, referred to as "Clippers," a term used to identify the airline's link to America's maritime heritage, and supported by generous postal contracts and the receipt of preferred mail routes, Pan American Airways quickly became the unofficial symbol of the nation's emerging air industry as its operations covered South and Central America, the Pacific, the Atlantic and major domestic routes. As it expanded its operations and as technology improved the size and performance of amphibious planes, the company added the Sikorsky S-42, the Martin M-130 and the Boeing B-314.

From its home base at Miami's Dinner Key, Pan Am ruled international air routes. The airline became synonymous with reliable, fast and luxurious travel. Where many domestic airlines used single-engine aircraft that could carry only ten to twelve passengers, the massive four-engine Clippers could carry thirty to forty passengers and two to three thousand pounds of freight and possessed a range of five hundred to nine hundred miles. Eventually, new developments in engine design that improved efficiency and power extended

Advertising pamphlet from Florida Airways extolling the virtues of air travel and detailing the personnel and equipment of this early Florida airline, circa 1928. *Wynne Collection.*

the range even farther. Passengers aboard Pan American Clippers enjoyed a level of luxury that rivaled that of most deluxe cars on railroads—sleeping berths, splendid meals and amenities dispensed by solicitous attendants. A trip on a Pan American Clipper was very different from a journey aboard one of the small local airlines that featured wicker seats crowded together with little in the way of comfort. Early airlines also had little sound insulation, and passengers found it difficult to enjoy their flight because of the constant loud drone of engines. In 1930, the nation's airlines attempted to alleviate some of the discomfort and mistrust of flying by adding stewards and stewardesses as part of their crews to provide food and drink services.

In 1934, George T. Baker founded National Airlines, a passenger airline backed by mail delivery contracts that was based at Albert Whitted Airport in St. Petersburg, although its limited operations used two small monoplanes at first, National soon expanded with the introduction of multi-engine planes like the Stinson Trimotor in 1935 and the Lockheed Electra (1937), the plane flown by Amelia Earhart and Fred Noonan on their ill-fated attempt to circumnavigate Earth. One of the hallmarks of National Airlines during its decades of operations was the introduction of new aircraft and the adoption of new technology as seen by its first use of jet airplanes for domestic flights in December 1958.

National Airlines operated in-state routes initially but soon expanded its operations to include other states. According to company statistics, the number of revenue passenger miles grew from some 250,000 miles in 1936 to more than 3 million in 1940. In 1939, the headquarters were moved from St. Petersburg to Jacksonville as the company continue to grow. Later, the headquarters

Above: Juan Terry Trippe, founder of Pan American World Airways, established the airline as the leader in providing overseas and around-the-world commercial flights using the legendary "Clipper" amphibious airplanes. *Pan American.*

Opposite: Pan American Airways, based on Dinner Key in Miami, utilized long-distance "Clipper" amphibious planes to establish a worldwide American airline that stressed speed, safety and comfort to passengers. *Library of Congress.*

were again relocated, this time to Miami's International Airport. National Airlines remained a major domestic carrier until 1980, when it was acquired by Pan Am. The need for larger and more efficient aircraft was a constant faced by all airlines, American and foreign, and aircraft manufacturers did not disappoint. The decades of the 1920s and 1930s were years in which the number of manufacturers and the types of aircraft proliferated. Not only were new aircraft introduced at a steady pace during this period, but aircraft safety also improved dramatically with the introduction of new communications and navigation equipment for planes and airports. Each year, aircraft manufacturers introduced new models that offered more passenger seats, greater cargo capacity and longer distances that could be covered. In addition, federal regulations calling for new safety features such as two-way radios, loop antennas and night navigation equipment made annual updating mandatory. Although the government subsidized the addition of these safety features, airlines, even the most successful ones, were forced to spend a large part of their annual revenue meeting these demands because the subsidies did not fully cover the costs.

The federal government assisted emerging airlines in another way. The National Weather Service, which had its origins as a civilian organization of

The Pan American headquarters on Miami's Dinner Key offered overseas passengers a state-of-the-art facility while waiting for arrivals and departures and modern, up-to-date maintenance shops to ensure the safety of aircraft operated by the company. *Library of Congress.*

Image of a 1926 United Airlines biplane over a trailer park, Bayshore Gardens, Manatee County, 1979. *Manatee County Public Library.*

volunteers in the late 1840s and later a branch of the Army's Signal Corps, had first been designated a separate federal agency in October 1890. At the request of President Benjamin Harrison, Congress created the Weather Service, a civilian agency, as a bureau in the Department of Agriculture. Over the following decades, the bureau expanded its services to the public by providing weather forecasts that were telegraphed to various cities around the nation. In 1902, the Marconi Company began to send updated reports on weather conditions and projections to Cunard ships at sea. Because of the need for updated information and because of the growing interest in weather prediction as a profession, college and high school courses in meteorology grew increasingly popular, eventually resulting in degrees being awarded in the 1930s for the completion of a rigorous program of study.

In 1920, the American Meteorological Society, an organization of professional meteorologists, was formed and quickly established guidelines for the profession. Amateur volunteers from the Cooperative Observer Program continued to be an important part of a nationwide weather system, and some five thousand meteorological stations were operated. The development of the radiosonde, a small radio transmitter and other weather measuring instruments attached to a balloon, in the early part of the decade vastly improved the ability of forecasters to provide accurate weather assessments. The advent of commercial radio greatly aided the usefulness of the weather forecasts generated by the Weather Bureau. The first broadcast of weather information occurred on November 2, 1920, when KDKA, the first commercial radio station in the United States, added forecasts to its regular programming. Soon, weather reports became a standard feature of radio stations across the nation, a practice that continues today with radio and television stations. In the airlines industries, regular reports on the weather were included in the two-way communications with planes in the air.

The airlines industry was not the only beneficiary of these reports, as farmers, fishermen and ships at sea used the information to regulate their activities. Following the devastating hurricanes of 1926 and 1928 that ended the Florida Boom of the 1920s, the demand grew for advanced information on the destructive storms that would allow time to protect lives and property. Finally, a separate group within the Weather Bureau was established for the specific task of gathering information and predicting hurricanes, just a few months ahead of the destructive Labor Day Hurricane of 1936.

Rapid changes in technology and practices were occurring at airports as well. By the mid-1930s, many larger and busier airports had added

Introduced in 1933, the all-metal Boeing 247 revolutionized the American airlines industry because of its built-in safety features, speed and overall comfort for passengers. *Smithsonian Institution.*

control towers to regulate incoming and outgoing flights, extended concrete runways, lights for night landings and takeoffs, maintenance facilities and on-site fueling stations to ensure the rapid refilling of aircraft. Many of the physical upgrades to these airports were undertaken by the New Deal "make work" agencies of the Roosevelt administration, while municipalities, airlines and private investors footed the remaining costs.

Along with the advances in technology and the improvements to airports, aircraft manufacturers listened to the airlines as they called for planes with larger load carrying capacity. The small single-engine planes of the early 1920s and even the larger tri-motored planes of the early 1930s were not capable of carrying enough passengers to generate enough profit to sustain an airline. Among the first such aircraft was the Boeing 247, a revolutionary plane that incorporated what would rapidly become standard features of

The Ford tri-motor plane was a popular and reliable aircraft used by early airlines. Passengers were accommodated by wicker seats in an open and noisy passenger area that frequently reeked of gasoline fumes and engine exhaust. *Smithsonian Institution.*

airliners: retractable landing gear, autopilot, de-icing equipment, trim tabs and an all-aluminum frame and outer skin. The 247 also featured large engines in wing nacelles that provided enough power to allow it to fly from San Francisco to New York in 19.5 hours, a record-setting pace that was half the time required by its chief competitor, the Ford tri-motor. The 247's major drawback was that it could carry only ten passengers, which did little to improve the revenue line for possible customers.

The 247 was introduced to the general public at the 1933 World's Fair in Chicago and hailed as the future of American aviation. Boeing received an amazing initial order of sixty aircraft, but this order came from Boeing Air Transport, a part of United Airlines. The final production figures for the 247 were for only seventy-five planes because of the 1934 arrival of the Douglas DC-2, a slightly larger and more powerful plane that could carry twelve to fourteen passengers and included all of the latest technology available. The DC-2 was quickly adopted for use by Transworld Airlines (TWA) and by Pan American Airways and constituted a large part of their inventory through 1938. It was also purchased by the United States military and modified for use as a transport.

Although a successful model for Douglas, the DC-2 enjoyed only a brief run as the best commercial aircraft. One model, the Douglas Sleeper

Douglas Aircraft Company, noting the success of the Boeing 247, introduced the DC series in 1934, and it quickly replaced the 247 as the airliner of choice. The DC-2 provided more passenger space, upgraded technology and more powerful engines. The DC-2's dominancy was short-lived and gave way to the ultimate supremacy of the civilian version of the DC-3 in 1936. *Trans World Airlines.*

Transport, originally designed to provide sleeping accommodations for transcontinental passengers, evolved into the DC-3, which could carry thirty-two passengers and was placed into service in 1936. The DC-3 was the first airliner that provided enough passenger space to make a profit for the airlines and helped them to continue operations without government subsidies. Able to fly from Los Angeles to New York in only sixteen hours, the rapid turnaround allowed airlines to stabilize prices at an affordable rate of $160 for a one-way ticket and $288 for a round-trip one.

By 1940, the DC-3 had become the industry standard operating plane, and by the time the production of the civilian version ended in 1942, some 607 units had been produced. The reliability and load capacity of the DC-3 attracted the attention of the world's militaries, which quickly adopted it for transport duty. The C-47, as the military version was known, was the most widely used aircraft during World War II and continued to be produced throughout the war years under license from Douglas by factories in Russia and Great Britain. Even the Japanese, who had been granted a license to manufacture the DC-2, produced a version of the plane. As late as the Vietnam War, the C-47 was used by the United States as the platform for its "Puff the Magic Dragon" gunship. More than 16,000 military versions of the DC-3 were eventually produced.

Improvements in aircraft and services provided by airlines produced results. The number of passengers rose from only 6,000 passengers in 1929 to more than 450,000 by 1934. By 1938, the number of air passengers had risen to more than 1.2 million, and the number increased each year after that. Still, only a tiny fraction of the traveling public flew.

But what of Florida? Like the rest of America, Floridians were caught up in the flying craze. Numerous small landing fields were carved out of vacant pasturelands and golf courses. The early 1920s saw an explosion in land values in the Sunshine State as the boom got underway. Florida was the new Promised Land, and after 1917–18, when it lost approximately

The DC-3 quickly became the most produced aircraft in the world after it was adopted as a transport by the United States military and Allied armies in World War II. Designated the C-41, more than sixteen thousand were produced, and some two hundred are still operational today. *American Airlines.*

3.5 percent of its population, the next two decades saw the number of Floridians explode. By 1922, more than 1 million people called the state home, and by 1926, at the peak of the boom, the number had increased to 1.4 million. Developers took advantage of newspapers and radio to advertise the virtues of moving to Florida, and Sunday newspapers were filled with glowing accounts of how the Florida lifestyle—sunshine, beaches, oceans, plentiful land, golf courses, modern homes and cosmopolitan cities—was the wave of the future. Colorful posters in the latest Art Deco style featured men and women living an idealized existence in the Sunshine State. Prominently displayed were the various means of getting to Florida—trains, automobiles, boats and planes. Newspapers also featured stories about the arrival of prominent people by airplane and their departures overseas. Pictures of planes and people were front-page news!

FLORIDA POPULATION, SELECTED YEARS, 1916–43

Year	*Population*
1916	924,000
1917	895,000
1918	865,000
1925	1,264,000
1926	1,368,000
1935	1,613,000
1940	1,915,000
1943	2,451,000

Source: U.S. Census Bureau

Although virtually every town had an airport of some kind and several successful interstate and international airlines operated in the state, the reality was that the majority of the newcomers to the state came by railroad. The fixed routes and the limited number of destinations served by railroads meant that these once dominant carriers would soon lose out to the cheaper and more flexible travel by automobiles. Just as the railroads had replaced steamboats and sailing vessels as major forms of transportation, the railroads were slowly losing their importance to the proliferating numbers of cars and trucks. Even during the depths of the Great Depression, Florida's population continued to grow, though slowly. By 1940, the state could claim more than 1.9 million citizens, and by 1943,

Left: Henry Flagler—petroleum magnate, hotelier and railroad entrepreneur—is often credited with starting the Florida Boom by pushing his Florida East Coast Railway along the state's eastern coast, while Henry Bradley Plant is credited with doing the same thing through the state's center and along the western coast. *Library of Congress.*

Right: Henry Bradley Plant, owner of the Plant System of railroads, and Flagler provided the means by which most people traveled to Florida during the boom. *Florida Memory.*

the population had grown to 2.5 million, fueled by the influx of trainees for America's armed forces.

World War II and the growing emphasis on airpower would dramatically affect the future of air travel in Florida as people became accustomed to seeing airplanes of all types in the clear skies of Florida.

COMMERCIAL AIRLINES AND THE BOOM

Someday Florida is going to be the greatest winter air travel market in the country. Who the hell wants to spend thirty hours getting there on a train when they can fly from New York to Miami in a third that time?
—Eddie Rickenbacker

Florida was the place to be in the 1920s. The population was rapidly expanding, thanks in part to soldiers returning from the Great War, but also the promise of untold fortunes in real estate speculation. Stories abounded "back home" of people doubling and tripling their investments in only a matter of days. It was all too good to pass up, and thousands of people moved to Florida during the decade looking to cash in.

U.S. Census Bureau statistics show that the population of Florida grew from just over 968,000 in 1920 to more than 1,468,000 in 1930, an incredible increase of more than 51 percent. Further showing the change is the shift from rural to urban living. In 1920, urban areas of Florida accounted for only 37 percent of residents compared to nationally 51 percent of the population being urban:

Year	*Florida Population*	*% Rural*	*# Rural*	*% Urban*	*# Urban*
1900	528,542	80%	421,511	20%	107,031
1910	752,619	71%	533,530	29%	219,089
1920	968,470	63%	612,645	37%	355,825
1930	1,468,211	48%	708,433	52%	759,778

Source: U.S. Census Bureau

By 1930, Florida's urban population had risen to 52 percent, a tremendous increase when coupled with the dramatic increase in population, while nationally, the urban population had increased to 56 percent. Florida was not just growing in numbers, and the rural way of life as a percentage of population was in rapid decline.

While water and rail had been the leading methods of transportation in the early growth years of Florida, the automobile was becoming a leader in bringing new populations to Florida. To accommodate this change, roads and bridges were constructed throughout the state. William B. Stronge pointed out the need for bridges to cut travel time and distance in a rapidly moving economy. When the Gandy Bridge was completed in 1924, it cut the travel distance from Tampa to St. Petersburg from forty-three miles to a much more traveler-friendly nineteen miles.

This increase in population led to many new opportunities in Florida. Jobs were readily available in the tourism and service industries, including hotels, restaurants, bars and other social venues. Skilled construction workers were in high demand, and as the real estate industry continued to expand, sales jobs were available, particularly in boom areas such as South Florida. It was not uncommon for a real estate broker to poach successful salespeople from other sellers with an offer of more money or perhaps a stake in land.

Men such as the architect Addison Cairns Mizner; his less successful brother, Wilson; sewing machine heir Paris Singer; and a young Florida-raised dreamer, George Merrick, would play prominent roles in the development of Florida during the boom years. Addison Mizner designed some of the grandest homes in South Florida, earning a reputation for his personal vision and ability to exceed the expectations of his clients. Singer was known for his Everglades Club in Palm Beach and his plans for a community he wished to call Palm Beach Ocean. Merrick, the son of a Congregationalist minister, dreamed of a community geared more toward the middle-class buyer—Coral Gables was born. As would be expected during heady days like these, there was a seedy underbelly as well. Unscrupulous speculators would prey on the unsuspecting and gullible. Properties were often sold multiple times in a day, increasing in price each time. Northerners, some seeking a retirement haven and some seeking a get-rich-quick opportunity, were unfamiliar with land in Florida and could be persuaded to purchase actual swampland.

Journalist Christopher Knowlton pointed out that the party lifestyle proved a prime factor not just in luring potential investors but also in attracting undesirables to the state. The illegal liquor trade was highly profitable. Rumrunners, while risking jail time, turned exceptional profits for their risk.

Left: Addison Cairns Mizner was the architect of choice for the wealthy new residents of Palm Beach and Boca Raton during the early 1920s. *Florida Memory.*

Right: A typical advertisement from the 1920s for land in Florida by Bunnell State Bank in the *Flagler Tribune,* March 12, 1925. *Flagler County Historical Society.*

Bars, nightclubs and hotels in turn sold this liquor at even higher prices. With illegal liquor came the criminal element of men such as Al Capone, who arrived in South Florida bringing with him gambling and prostitution.

Florida seemed to have unlimited growth potential, and while the Great Depression and the land bust caused considerable financial harm to many, including those aforementioned real estate barons, some American businesses continued to expand. Although it may not have been smooth flying, industries such as airlines, used both for airmail and passenger traffic, began to secure a firm foothold in the state of Florida. Several airlines still familiar to us today got their start, or expanded dramatically, during these turbulent years, often by taking advantage of government incentives and by filling unmet consumer expectations.

In 1925, Congress passed the Kelly Act. This act transferred the carrying of airmail to private contractors. An early beneficiary of this change was Pitcairn Aviation. Pitcairn Aviation was the brainchild of Harold Pitcairn and Agnew Lawson. Their original aircraft was built as a racing plane, allowing them to be able to move quickly and provide services across the Eastern Seaboard.

Upon passage of the Kelly Act, Pitcairn placed successful bids for several delivery contracts and went into the mail delivery business. Pitcairn's first contract included mail delivery from New Jersey to Atlanta. In December 1918, this contract was extended almost six hundred miles, tasking the company with mail delivery to Miami, including several stops along the route. For Florida, this provided the first airmail service to Orlando on March 1, 1929.

The business proved short-lived, however, and Pitcairn Aviation was sold to Clement Keys and North American Aviation, in 1929. By 1930, Keys had changed the name of the business to Eastern Air Transport, relocated the company headquarters to Brooklyn and started flying passengers. In 1932, a one-way ticket from Newark, New Jersey, to Miami cost $74, while a round-trip ticket cost $131.20. The two-and-a-half-hour trip from Tampa

Pitcairn Aviation, which eventually formed the foundation for Eastern Airlines, successfully operated its "mailwing" until changes by the Postal Service reduced the subsidies paid for delivering airmail. *Smithsonian Institution.*

Left: Clement Melville Keys, a Canadian-born financier, played an important role in American aviation during the 1920s and 1930s. He acquired Pitcairn Aviation when it went bankrupt in 1929 and sold its shares to North American Aviation two weeks later. North American Aviation eventually morphed into Eastern Airlines. *Smithsonian Institution.*

Below: Eastern Airlines had ticket offices in major hotels and in downtown locations. The Temple Terrace Hotel (Tampa) offered this convenient service to its clients. *Robertson-Fresh Collection.*

to Jacksonville, including a fifteen-minute layover in Daytona Beach, cost passengers $13.98.

In 1933, Eastern offered New York passengers a nearly fourteen-hour flight to Miami, including stops in Richmond and Jacksonville. While not convenient by modern standards, this flight time was still less than a modern train ride from New York to Miami, which Amtrak estimates at twenty-eight to thirty-three hours depending on the train.

Keys was also an innovator in the use of what we now call flight attendants but at the time were called hostesses. In the 1930s, however, things were quite different. Eastern had set guidelines for the type of women it would hire as a hostess. Hostesses were required to be under age twenty-eight and to be single. There were height and weight guidelines that women were required to meet. Hostesses were to be either a college graduate or a registered nurse.

While Keys was making improvements to Eastern, the realities of the Great Depression could not keep the airline profitable. In 1933, General Motors purchased a controlling interest in North American Aviation, merging it with the General Aviation Manufacturing Corporation. In 1935, Captain Eddie Rickenbacker, the World War I fighter ace with twenty-six air battle victories to his name and recipient of the Medal of Honor, came on as general manager. Rickenbacker understood the potential of Florida air travel, having been quoted as saying, "Someday Florida is going to be the greatest winter air travel market in the country. Who the hell wants to spend thirty hours getting there on a train when they can fly from New York to Miami in a third that time?"

With Rickenbacker at the helm, Eastern passenger traffic grew from roughly seven thousand in 1934 to more than twelve thousand in 1935, an astounding leap considering the country was still in the worst years of the Great Depression. Rickenbacker was even able to turn a small profit—from a loss of $1.5 million in 1934 to a small but not insignificant profit of $38,000 in 1935. It was in 1935 that Rickenbacker relocated the Eastern Airlines headquarters to Miami, a move that paid dividends for both the airline and the city for many years.

General Motors made the decision to separate Eastern from its North American Aviation Corporation in 1937, and Eastern was put on the market. With some behind-the-scenes maneuvering, Rickenbacker acquired a purchase option at $3.5 million, equivalent to roughly $74 million today. Rickenbacker was able to raise the funds over thirty days, with the help of Kuhn, Loeb and Company, and in 1938 became the president of a growing airline. For his money, Rickenbacker acquired twenty-two planes (including

An American International Airways passenger plane at Tampa's Drew Field on January 7, 1930. *Burgert Brothers Photographic Collection.*

ten DC-2s, ten DC-3s and two Stinson Reliant trainers), 3,692 route miles and the obligation of being the employer of more than 900 persons.

Rough times were ahead. Along with Rickenbacker taking control of Eastern, Germany invaded Austria. Already a military man, Rickenbacker understood Eastern's obligations, and during World War II, the airline organized part of its fleet into a "Military Air Transport Division," carrying 60 million pounds of cargo and more than 125,000 military passengers in support of the war effort.

In 1919, a twenty-eight-year-old Naval Reserve pilot by the name of Juan Terry Trippe, in an article for the *Graphic*, an illustrated literary magazine published at Yale University, stated prophetically, "A flight across the Atlantic is a perfectly safe and sane commercial proposition and not a gigantic gamble." Pan American Airways, better known as Pan Am, a company Trippe served as CEO of for four decades, was to become an innovator and leader in transporting international travelers.

Trippe learned to fly in the navy during World War I. After the war, he attended Yale University, becoming a founding member of the Yale Flying Club. Soon after graduation, he started the short-lived Long Island Airways, a sightseeing and taxi service for wealthy New York residents. Despite this setback, Trippe would not be out of the industry for long. Calling on Yale friends Cornelius Vanderbilt Whitney, William Vanderbilt and John Hambleton, he was able to start a small venture, Eastern Air Transport (separate from the business discussed prior), with the goal of acquiring airmail contracts. Having little success, Trippe merged his business with that of Colonial Airways, another airmail contract bidder. Not being in control galled Trippe, and he soon left the organization, again looking for a fresh start, only this time he had eyes on Florida and international routes.

Trippe's new company, Aviation Corporation of the Americas, was funded by himself, Hambleton, Whitney and other smaller investors, with a goal of securing the lucrative Key West to Havana, Cuba airmail route. Two other groups sought the same contract. Florida Airways, the brainchild of Reed Chambers and future Eastern Airlines executive Eddie Rickenbacker, proved a short-lived competitor, quickly closing operations in 1926 after several unfortunate crashes.

The third bidder was the more formidable Pan American Airways, with the backing of Sociedad Colombo Alemana de Transportes Aeros, a Colombian airline in business since 1921. Pan American Airways was able to secure the contract, much to the consternation of Trippe. While Pan American had the contract, it did not appear to have the physical assets to operate efficiently, nor did it have the support of the Cuban government.

Seeing his opportunity, Trippe suggested a merger between his own Aviation Corporation of the Americas and the rival Pan American Airways.

Pan American Airways admission ticket to the dedication of Tampa International Airport and the inauguration of the Tampa–Havana route on December 4, 1933. *Smithsonian Institution.*

A group photo including Postmistress Elizabeth Barnard and Tampa mayor Perry Wall (far right), with mail sacks, beside a Florida Airways mail plane at Drew Field, Tampa, April 1, 1926. *Burgert Brothers Photographic Collection.*

As talks moved slowly, Trippe visited Havana, where he was able to gain an audience with Cuban president Gerardo Machado. When Trippe returned to Florida, his Aviation Corporation held the landing rights in Havana, essentially making the Pan American contract worthless without the proposed merger. By mid-June 1927, Aviation Corporation of the Americas and Pan American Airways had come together in a merger out of business necessity. In 1931, the combined company took on the name Pan American Airways.

Despite the merger of the airmail delivery contract and landing rights, the first days for the new company proved difficult. The airline was still without the agreed-on planes. Its airmail contract stated that the first flight must occur by October 19, 1927, and on that date more than thirty thousand pieces of mail were awaiting delivery. Trippe's manager in Key West, J.E. Whitbeck, saved the day, chartering a Fairchild FC-2 floatplane to undertake the ninety-mile flight. This $175 expense possibly saved the contract and led to a long business life for Trippe and Pan American. Less than two weeks later, Trippe took delivery of two Fokker F-7 trimotor planes, ensuring that mail deliveries would be made according to contractual terms.

Another photograph of Tampa mayor Perry Wall and Postmistress Elizabeth Barnard receiving airmail from a Florida Airways plane at Drew Field in Tampa on April 1, 1926. *Burgert Brothers Photographic Collection.*

With the success of the Key West–Havana route, the company bid on other routes, focusing on Mexico and the Caribbean. It was during this period that Pan American moved its operations to Miami, allowing it to further focus on growth opportunities in Central and South America. In 1929 alone, mail and passenger service were offered to San Juan, Puerto Rico; Santiago, Chile; Paramaribo, Suriname; and other exotic locales.

Trippe's success was not lost in the media, and on July 31, 1933, he appeared on the cover of *TIME* magazine. This company-related celebrity status had been created even earlier in the decade through the hiring of Charles A. Lindbergh as a technical advisor. Trippe and Lindbergh began crafting plans for operating both Atlantic and Pacific routes, routes that would considerably lessen the time needed for both mail and human transport. Trippe's 1919 vision was coming to fruition.

Knowing that overseas flights were the future of international travel, Trippe and Lindbergh accepted bids from both Glenn L. Martin Company and Sikorsky Aero Engineering for planes to achieve the Pan American goal

The basis of the initial success of Pan American was its exclusive landing rights in Cuba and the resultant airmail contract. Passenger service, which had first been offered by the now defunct Aeromarine Airline, was also offered via the famous Clippers. *Smithsonian Institution.*

Pan American airport inspection team in Miami in 1932. *Florida Memory.*

of crossing the Pacific with passengers. Christened as a "Clipper Ship," the Martin M-130 was a four-engine plane that could haul forty-one passengers nearly three thousand miles. The *China Clipper* took to the air in November 1935 on a seven-day journey across the Pacific Ocean. The flight path departed from San Francisco, making stops in Honolulu, Midway Island, Wake Island and Guam before reaching the flight's destination in Manila. Passenger traffic across the Pacific was now a reality.

Trippe did not forget about his goal of passenger traffic crossing the Atlantic, and in a move that almost cost him control of Pan American, he put out a call for even larger Clipper Ships. The contract was awarded to Boeing for its new B-314, a huge plane in its day, seating seventy-four passengers with a range of approximately 3,500 miles at a speed of 180 miles per hour.

Problems beset the project from the beginning. Compounding financial losses on the Pacific routes, Boeing was late in delivering its new planes. The Pan American Board of Directors had lost patience and in 1939 placed Sonny Whitney in charge. Whitney proved no better suited in the

Pan American World Airways served as an unofficial instrument of American foreign policy by showing the country's flag in far-flung ports-of-call. The Clippers of the airline were always identified with the United States. *Smithsonian Institution.*

The Martin M-130, more popularly known as the "China Clipper," provided passengers with the same personal services—including sleeping berths—that travelers had grown accustomed to on America's finest railroad cars. *Pan American.*

mind of the board, and in early 1940, it restored Trippe. In May 1940, the first transatlantic mail flight occurred, and in June, passenger flights were undertaken. Passengers could now fly from New York to Marseilles aboard a comfortable Pan American Clipper Ship.

Success was to be brief, however, as the clouds of war grew darker in both the West and the East. Pan American assets were to prove vital in the war effort. During the war, Pan Am made more than nineteen thousand ocean crossing flights, carrying both men and supplies to far-reaching areas. The company helped build air bases and landing fields, while training more than five thousand pilots how to efficiently fly over open ocean.

George T. "Ted" Baker may seem an unusual entry to the world of aviation. Baker was a successful financier in Chicago when he happened upon a magazine ad for Detroit Aircraft Company, advertising Eastman flying boats. Baker had thought of owning a plane, and now he had the perfect opportunity. With Prohibition being the rule of the land, Baker used his newly purchased plane as an opportunity to create a charter air service he named National Airlines Air Taxi System. For several years, Baker had a thriving business, operating three planes, flying Chicagoans who were eager for a drink but unwilling to brave the illegal clubs, to Canada, where alcohol was still legal and quite inexpensive. With the passage of the Twenty-First Amendment in 1933, Prohibition came to an end, and so did much of Baker's passenger traffic. Chicago residents no longer needed to fly across the border for their favorite beverage. It could be purchased at the corner bar on demand.

By 1934, Ted Baker had found himself a resident of St. Petersburg, Florida, operating the renamed National Airlines System. When asked how he made his way to St. Petersburg, the young entrepreneur

The Boeing 314 Clipper, made famous by Pan American World Airways, on its different routes to exotic ports-of-call around the world. *Smithsonian Institution.*

The lobby of the Pan American terminal at Miami International Airport, featuring the famous globe that mapped the various routes the airline flew. *Smithsonian Institution.*

Right: George T. Baker, the founder of National Airlines, began his career in the airlines industry flying passengers seeking to avoid Prohibition in the United States into Canada. *Wynne Collection.*

Below: City officials and airline executives at the opening of the McMullin School of Aviation at Orlando Municipal Airport, circa 1930. *Smithsonian Institution.*

answered, "I didn't establish headquarters here simply by chance, but I did come here after months of careful map study had convinced me that St. Peterburg was one of the best transcontinental airports in the entire United States." Historian Thomas Reilly is quick to point out the fallacy in Baker's statement.

With the decline in alcohol-based travel, Baker had to find new revenue streams for his struggling business. He did so just as others had done: airmail. Baker was the successful bidder on Air Mail Route 31, a short trip across the state of Florida from St. Petersburg to Daytona Beach, with stops along the way in Tampa, Lakeland and Orlando. Baker arrived in Florida in September 1934 with two Ryan single-engine monoplanes and hopes of success. Baker's hopes for success began with his first flight on October 15 and required much hard, physical labor. Historian Warren J. Brown described the early days in St. Petersburg for Baker, as "he flew as pilot, sold tickets, and loaded the aircraft, far into the nights keeping the airline running."

Baker was to quickly learn the realities of the business. With Eastern declining to bid on Route 31, Baker and National were low bidders. His airmail delivery weights and contracted mileage were low; thus, his airmail payments were small. His planes were also small, seating only three passengers in addition to the pilot, so his ability to sell passenger seats was limited. Warren J. Brown estimated that National sold fewer than four hundred passenger seats its first year of operations. Baker had to find additional revenue streams to keep his planes flying.

Hoping to increase his flight miles, Baker requested to extend his flights to include a stop in Jacksonville after leaving Daytona Beach. This request was declined by the superintendent of the airmail division as being a duplicate of services already provided. Any mail that Baker delivered that was headed north or south was offloaded from his plane in Daytona Beach and placed on an Eastern Airlines plane, the company that held the contract for that route.

National and Baker were persistent, and maintenance at the Daytona Beach airport during early 1935 provided the opening National needed to expand, at least temporarily, to Jacksonville. Sources are not in agreement as to what was happening in Daytona Beach. Thomas Reilly, writing in *Tampa Bay History*, stated that an Eastern DC-2 aircraft flew into newly installed utility wires, causing the airport to shut down. Warren J. Brown, in his book, *Florida's Aviation History*, noted that Works Progress Administration crews were making improvements to the landing strips and that there was no traffic in or out of the airport. Contemporary newspaper accounts show that in July 1935, a nearly $43,000 project was awarded to Sholtz Field in Daytona Beach to complete runway work, including paving two 2,500-by-100-foot runways and installing drainage ditches and grass. This project appears to have been ongoing through the fall months. Whatever the reason, National and Eastern were unable to make connection in Daytona Beach, and airmail service was interrupted. The Postal Service had to step in and decide on a course of action.

Eddie Rickenbacker and Eastern were vocal in their opposition to National wedging its way into contracted routes. The Postal Service, however, granted temporary approval for Baker to fly mail and passengers to Jacksonville. There, mail could be handed off to Eastern for flights both north and south. A frustrated Rickenbacker had little recourse, while Baker and National were able to expand their reach and grow revenue. When the Daytona Beach airport reopened, National's approval to fly to Jacksonville was continued with slight modifications to not duplicate Eastern's route. National would be required to service DeLand and Sanford, further expanding the fledgling airlines reach.

An airliner (probably a DC-2) in front of the Peter O. Knight Airport Administration Building on Davis Island, Tampa, 1939. *Burgert Brothers Photographic Collection.*

National Airlines' southern routes were designated the "Buccaneer Routes" after Eddie Rickenbacker, the head of Eastern Airlines, accused Baker of pirating airmail routes from Eastern. *Wikimedia Commons.*

The personal battle between Baker and Rickenbaker took a mildly humorous turn when the Eastern executive called Baker and National a bunch of pirates. Not one to let this slide, Baker used it to his advantage, rolling out a new National logo and catchphrase for his service: "The Buccaneer Route."

As National's fortunes slowly improved, Baker recognized the need for larger aircraft to fly the increasing number of passengers and the larger volume of mail. Baker borrowed money from his Chicago-based friend Harry Parker and purchased two used Stinson SM-6000 tri-motor planes. These planes had an eight-passenger capacity and led Baker to hire a flight attendant, Charlotte Georgia. Georgia's role was much different than we are used to today. In a *St. Petersburg Times* article, she recounted, "We didn't serve any food, didn't have restrooms. I used to tell passengers where we were, pass out cigarettes, gum, magazines."

On May 15, 1930, Ellen Church led the first group of what were then called "hostesses" or "stewardesses" on a Boeing Air Transport (United Airlines) flight. Church and three other young women served as flight attendants on flights from San Francisco to Chicago, which took twenty hours and thirteen stops for fourteen passengers. *Smithsonian Institution.*

INFORMATION—RESERVATIONS—TICKETS

GROUND TRANSPORTATION

CITY—AIRPORT—FARE

GENERAL INFORMATION

CORRECTED TO NOVEMBER 1, 1938

SERVING

NEW ORLEANS
JACKSONVILLE
MIAMI
MOBILE
SARASOTA
MARIANNA
LAKELAND
ST. PETERSBURG
NATIONAL AIRLINES
PENSAC
FT. MY
GULFP
ORLANI
TALLAHASSEE
DAYTONA BEACH

U.S. AIRMAIL-PASSENGERS-AIR EXPR

NOV 17 1938

Above: The Stinson SM-3000, a tri-motor passenger plane, could carry eight passengers and was the main plane used by National Airlines in its first years of operation. *Wikimedia Commons.*

Left: National Airlines focused its business on cities in Florida and along the Gulf Coast, although it did fly to the Northeast. This 1938 brochure lists the cities served. *National Airlines.*

The Stinson aircraft helped push passenger traffic at National to new heights. From a start of 400 passengers in 1934 and 887 in 1935, National recorded passenger traffic of more than 1,600 in 1936. Mail deliveries were on the rise also, from less than 7,100 pounds in 1935 to more than 10,600 pounds in 1936. The year 1937 saw a merger with Gulf Airlines, the resulting company taking the name National Airlines. The same year saw the inauguration of passenger flights from St. Petersburg and Tampa to Miami, with stops in Sarasota and Fort Myers. The two-hour flight from St. Petersburg to Miami cost $14.70.

In the fall of 1937, National purchased four Lockheed L-10 Electra airplanes, two new and two used. This growth, and the arrival of small unregulated competitors, led Baker to examine all aspects of his business, including employee attire. National introduced an employee uniform consisting of dark-blue serge suits, along with blue shirts and a necktie. It would be easy now to distinguish a National Airlines employee. Baker understood the importance of a professional image to potential clients.

Still looking to expand, in 1938 National Airlines was awarded the potentially lucrative Jacksonville–New Orleans airmail route 39 contract. This should have been a tremendous boost to National, but it came at a cost. National was still flying from Daytona Beach to Jacksonville on a temporary basis, and that year the Postal Service withdrew this authorization. Now Baker was left with two separate, non-connected routes. It would be two years until Baker was able to convince the newly created Civil Aeronautics Authority to restore the Daytona–Jacksonville route, in effect creating one long route for National, including growing cities such as Miami, Tampa, Orlando, Pensacola, Mobile and New Orleans.

In a brief five-year period, Ted Baker, a financier by trade, had turned a small outfit helping Chicago residents evade Prohibition to a growing airline that had taken on Eddie Rickenbacker in a turf battle and won, to a company that in 1980 would merge with Pan American World Airways, providing the primarily international carrier a domestic presence in the United States.

The "boom" years of the 1920s leading into the years of the Great Depression were difficult for most Floridians, but this period was crucial to aviation history, not just in the state but to the United States as a whole. New companies were born out of the entrepreneurial spirit that characterizes Americans. The expansion of airmail through private carriers allowed millions to send and receive letters from friends and family across the country in a comparatively safe, quick and inexpensive manner. Cagey businessmen turned the delivery of mail into opportunities to also "deliver" passengers.

The Pan American Headquarters building on Dinner Key was utilized as the city hall for Miami after the company went out of business in December 1991. *Library of Congress.*

While air travel was out of the reach of most Floridians, those with the financial ability were able to cross the state almost at will.

While the end of the 1930s saw a light toward the end of the Great Depression tunnel, there were other clouds on the horizon. Aggression in both the West and the East would lead to an unprecedented war—a war that would not be winnable without air power. Florida would be called on and play a role much larger than anticipated during what came to be World War II. It would have a crucial role to play in the economic development of the state in the years immediately after the end of hostilities.

FLORIDA

The Floating Fortress

Underlying the statute [Civil Aeronautics Act] *is the principle that the country's welfare in time of peace and its safety in time of war rests upon the existence of a stabilized aircraft production—an economically and technically sound air transportation system, both domestic and overseas—an adequate supply of well trained civilian pilots and ground personnel.*
—Franklin Delano Roosevelt, January 24, 1939

The turbulent rise and fall of many airline companies in the 1920s and 1930s was of growing concern to President Franklin D. Roosevelt, his advisors and the business community in the United States. Even a casual observation of the evolution of commercial airlines in Europe and the extent to which European governments encouraged technological and service expansion through indirect or direct subsidies to aircraft manufacturers and airlines revealed how far America was lagging behind. Because the American military was solely dependent on aircraft produced by civilian companies, the nation's military aircraft was woefully inadequate when compared with those operated by potential adversaries in future wars. Aircraft manufacturers—watching the same military events taking place in Asia, Africa and Europe—designed new planes on their own, but funds to purchase the new aircraft were not forthcoming from Congress. Manufacturing facilities to build new planes were small and slow, and industrialists were reluctant to invest the funds needed to create larger, faster and more efficient factories.

Not only was the United States lagging in technological development, but the nation also faced critical shortages in the infrastructure that would accommodate newer aircraft. In Florida in 1938, there were only three military airports: Eglin Army Air Field, Pensacola Naval Air Station and Naval Reserve Training Base Miami. The lack of more bases was indicative of the small size of the American military in the 1930s. The entire armed forces in 1939—U.S. Army, Navy, Marine Corps and Coast Guard—numbered only 334,473 persons, which placed it thirty-ninth overall in size compared to the armed forces of other nations. A series of reductions in personnel followed the end of World War I and continued throughout the 1920s and the first half of the 1930s. The total number of military aircraft available for service was fewer than three thousand, and aircraft manufacturers were producing only three hundred new planes each year for the U.S. Army, Navy and Marine Corps.

Divisive American politics—such as the isolationist movement led by William Borah, Gerald P. Nye and Robert LaFollette—created a formidable barrier for newly elected president Franklin D. Roosevelt, who viewed the rise of Fascist dictatorships in Europe and the aggression of Japan in the Far East as harbingers of future wars that would almost certainly involve the United States. As a result, Roosevelt utilized various make-work programs of the New Deal to strengthen the infrastructure needed to accommodate an expanded military. The Works Progress Administration, the Public Works Administration and the Civilian Conservation Corps had cooperated with local municipalities in building or expanding airports in smaller towns and cities to encourage airlines to develop new routes and expand their services. The passage of the Civil Aeronautics Act of 1939 provided the necessary structure for improving the operations of commercial flights.

For the military, particularly the navy, the creation of the Hepburn Board in June 1938, a fact-finding commission chaired by Admiral Arthur Japy Hepburn, was a critical turning point after years of neglect and paltry funding. The members of the board represented the new crop of naval leaders who focused their attention on expanding the air arm of the navy and were charged with evaluating existing naval facilities, recommending new bases and updating the overall strategy of the navy. Roosevelt, who participated in massive fleet exercises off the coast of Cuba the same month, had begun the task of revamping and modernizing the navy when he had visited the largely abandoned base at Key West and was agreeable to the recommendations it made.

The Hepburn Board, although emphasizing the growing threat of Japanese expansion in the Pacific and the need to concentrate the Pacific Fleet at Pearl Harbor, Hawaii, also recognized the need to afford protection to the extended Atlantic coastline, and from this need, Florida was a major beneficiary. The board recommended the reactivation and modernization of the Key West base, which would allow the United States to project its naval power from Florida southward to the coasts of Central and South America. In addition, the Hepburn Board called for the creation of three major naval pilot training bases in the continental States, including major upgrades to the existing training facilities at Pensacola.

The major focus of the board in Florida was the creation of new bases for seaplanes operations in the Atlantic that would provide surveillance and, if necessary, offensive options as needed. A new seaplane base was recommended for the barrier island across the Indian River Lagoon from the city of Melbourne, which would allow the navy to control the ocean from mid-Florida to the Straights of Cuba. Perhaps the most important of the board's recommendations for the Sunshine State involved the development of its Mayport facility for aircraft carrier operations and the purchase of the Florida National Guard's Camp J. Clifford R. Foster (formerly Camp Joseph E. Johnston) at Black Point on the St. Johns River for use by navy land-based fighters, bombers and surveillance aircraft. The Florida National Guard would find a new home on seventy thousand acres in rural Clay County, which by late 1940 had been transformed into a modern infantry training base. Between 1940 and 1945, more than 1.5 million soldiers would receive their training there.

As soon as the board was finished with its survey and formalized its recommendations, the president began implementing them. In early 1939, a group of thirteen navy personnel made their way to Brevard County to begin the initial construction of the new Banana River Naval Air Station. The State of Florida and the federal government completed negotiations to transfer Camp Foster to the navy. Navy planes were immediately based at Black Point, and construction began on the new Jacksonville Naval Air Station. Harbor improvements were made to the Mayport facility, and a patrol torpedo boat (PT boat) detachment was assigned there to protect the coastline.

Three major centers in Florida, California and Virginia provided naval pilot training as the navy began to shift its offensive strategy from battleships to aircraft carriers in response to Japan's increasing use of them in the Pacific. While naval appropriations had been somewhat curtailed during the

Camp Joseph E. Johnston, named for the famous Confederate general, was located at Black Point on the St. Johns River near Jacksonville. It was not set up to accommodate pilot training, so the army established a training airfield at Clewiston. These two soldiers were getting familiar with driving a huge military truck as the American armed forces moved to mechanization in 1918. *Wynne Collection.*

Depression by 1940, the American navy could boast seven carriers, although only three were originally designed as carriers. Rigid dirigibles, although diminishing in importance as offensive weapons, continued to be included in the navy's arsenal, and a training facility operated at Lakehurst, New Jersey.

The principal training base for the Army Air Corps was located at Randolph Field, Brooks Field and Kelly Field near San Antonio, Texas. The first class to graduate from the program at Randolph Field numbered only 257 individuals. The concern of American officials about the situation in Europe also resulted in a decision to allow private aviation schools to begin training army pilots for combat, a ploy to secure qualified pilots while maintaining the appearance of neutrality. This decision was made by General Henry H. "Hap" Arnold, who, when Congressional funds for expanded training were not forthcoming, convened a conference with owners of private companies; by early 1939, nine private schools had been contracted with by the Army Air Corps, a number that soon expanded to fifty-six within a short period. "The Air Corps paid the contract schools a fee for each graduate, initially $1,170, and furnished the airplanes, a cadre of supervisory personnel, textbooks, and flying clothing for the students," noted air force historian Bruce A. Ashcroft. "The accident rates at the schools were lower than the historical average at Randolph, and student elimination rates compared favorably." By 1941, the Army Air Corps had contracted with forty-five private companies, and by 1945, the number had increased to sixty-three.

The passage of the Selective Service Act of 1940 brought 900,000 Americans into the military for one year of training. The influx of such large numbers made the recommendations of the Hepburn Board and planners from other federal agencies critical to building new facilities to accommodate them. The limited number of training centers operated by the American military could not adequately handle the large numbers of new recruits, and new facilities had to be developed. Because the process of expropriating land to build new bases or to expand older ones could be a time-consuming exercise, the federal government turned to projects that had their origins in the make-work programs of the New Deal to quickly construct facilities for the new recruits.

In Florida, the new National Guard base near Starke in Clay County, which encompassed some 170,000 acres by that point, was large enough to handle entire divisions, but to ensure an even greater capacity for the training of ground troops, negotiations for the expropriation of land for another large base began in Franklin County and vicinity. Some 165,000 acres of land near Carrabelle and Lanark would become an amphibious training base for the army. Together, these two bases, along with the Underwater Demolition and Amphibious schools at Fort Pierce, would train more than 2 million infantry and amphibious troops for service in the European and Pacific Theaters. The total number of infantry recruits trained in Florida vastly outnumbered the state's permanent population in 1940.

As important as the army infantry training centers were, it was the aviation training centers in the Sunshine State that dominated the military importance of Florida. In 1939, there were only 9 federal military bases in the state, including three airfields. At the end of 1945, just a mere six years later, there were 190 of various sizes and with different purposes. While the army training centers operated in limited spaces in rural areas far removed from major population centers, the army and navy aviation bases were often located with a few miles' proximity of towns and major cities, and Florida residents became familiar with seeing airplanes of all descriptions and sizes operating in the skies above them. By 1945, the navy had 20 naval stations plus auxiliary fields, in operation, while the army could claim 47 training bases, along with multiple bombing and gunnery ranges:

Main Army Pilot Training Bases in Florida, 1939–45
United States Army, Civilian Pilot Schools, British Flight Training

Alachua AAF
Drew AAF
MacDill AAF
Orlando AAF
Apalachicola AAF
Dunnellon AAF
Marianna AAF
Chapman CPS
Avon Park AAF
Eglin AAF
Miami AAF
Avon Park CPS
Fort Myers AAF (Paige Field)
Montbrook (Williston) AAF
Bartow AAF
Hendricks AAF
Morrison AAF
Boca Chica AAF
Hillsborough AAF
Naples AAF
Boca Raton AAF
Homestead AAF
Ocala CPS
Brooksville AAF
Jacksonville AAF
Perry AAF
Buckingham AAF
Keystone AAF
Pinecastle AAF
Carlstrom CPS
Kissimmee AAF
Punta Gorda AAF
Clewiston BFT
Lakeland AAF
Tyndall AAF
Dale Mabry AAF
Lakeland CPS
Venice AAF
Dorr AAF
Leesburg AAF
Zephyrhills AAF

Legend
AAF = Army Air Fields
CPS = Civilian Pilot Schools
BFT = British Flight Training

Source: Compiled from Anthony Atwood, "A State of War: Florida from 1939 to 1945," PhD dissertation, Florida International University, 2012.

In order to regulate the increasing number of airplanes flown by members of the different entities at one time, the federal authorities roughly divided the Florida peninsula into three spheres of control. Because the navy maintained bases that were actively engaged in conducting defensive operations while also engaging in pilot training, it was given overall responsibility for the Atlantic coast. The coastline was subdivided into three major administrative commands: Jacksonville south to Cape Canaveral, Cape Canaveral south to Fort Lauderdale and Fort Lauderdale south to Miami. The navy was also given responsibility for defensive operations in the Straights of Cuba and south in the Caribbean to South America. The refurbished base at Key West was the administrative hub for this section. Because one of the primary instruction sites for carrier pilots was in Pensacola, the navy was also given the responsibility for defending the Gulf of Mexico. Responsibility for the central part of the peninsula belonged to the army.

Naval Air Stations for Defense and Pilot Training, 1939–46

NAS Banana River	NAS Jacksonville
NAAS Barin Field	NAS Key West
NAAS Bronson Field	NAS Lake City
NAAS Cecil Field	NAS Mayport
NAAS Corey Field	NAS Melbourne
NAS Daytona Beach	NAS Miami
NAS DeLand	NAS Pensacola
NAF Dinner Key	NAS Richmond
NAAS Ellyson Field	NAS Sanford
NAS Fort Lauderdale	NAAS Saufley Field
NAAS Green Cove Springs	NAS Vero Beach
NAAS JAX Municipal No. 1	NAAS Whiting Field

Source: Compiled from Anthony Atwood, "A State of War: Florida from 1939 to 1945," PhD dissertation, Florida International University, 2012.

The boundaries of each of these zones were not carved in stone, and planes and pilots from the army and the navy operated in all areas, sharing airspace and missions. Although Florida was sparsely populated and had plenty of open land, most bases were located in proximity to the Atlantic Ocean or the Gulf of Mexico for three reasons. German U-boats preyed on Allied shipping in the waters close to the peninsula, and thus Florida was on the front lines of the war. Indeed, in June 1942, the state had, along with Long Island, been invaded by Nazi saboteurs at Ponte Vedra Beach. The second reason was to force pilots to learn to rely on instrument navigation since few landmarks could be found over the open water. Lastly, the large numbers of military aircraft mandated that the different services develop and utilize a system of control that crossed the lines of service organization.

Service crews and a Curtiss flying boat at Pensacola Naval Air Station during World War I. *Florida Memory.*

The close juxtaposition of military bases in Florida created an ideal climate to foster cooperation between rival service branches. In his analysis of the military operations in the Sunshine State, Anthony D. Atwood noted:

> *Florida's experience in the war was in some respects a model of joint service and the absence of rivalry. The twenty naval air stations and forty-seven Army airfields of Florida worked together within the peninsula's airspace to create air forces that were as capable of reducing powerful industrial states, as they were at controlling the 70 percent of the world that is water. Navy instructors from Pensacola helped train the Doolittle Raiders at Eglin. Army pilots from MacDill helped fly the ASW patrols that drove back the U-boats. At the amphibious training centers of Camp Gordon Johnston and Fort Pierce, tens of thousands of soldiers and sailors trained together on all aspects of littoral warfare in relative harmony. During the several years of the military reorganization following World War II, Florida's experience was an example of joint service cooperation.*

Some of the bases included elements from all of the services undergoing a common training program or having specific courses open to all branches.

The Underwater Demolition and Amphibious Landing Base at Fort Pierce was a good example of interservice cooperation. In 1943, the army's amphibious training program at Camp Gordon Johnston had been shut down, and army personnel and equipment were transferred to the Fort Pierce base. Some 150,000 U.S. Marine Corps, Navy and Army personnel were trained there. Camp Gordon Johnston and Camp Blanding offered jungle survival courses to navy personnel, along with parachute training for some other service units.

The Marine Corps provided familiarization courses to army personnel on the "Roebling Alligator" at its base in Dunnellon. The Alligator, developed as an all-terrain vehicle to rescue hurricane victims in the Everglades during the 1930s by Donald Roebling, was considered an ideal landing craft and was used by Allied armies and navies in both the European and Pacific Theaters. It caught the attention of the Marine Corps in 1937 when it was featured in a story in *Life* magazine. The service branch quickly began experiments with the Alligator, adapting different turrets and weapons to the hull and modifying landing tactics to fit the abilities of the machine. It was developed in Florida and manufactured in the Sunshine State in factories in Dunnellon and Lakeland.

The army, too, had its own landing craft that it shared with the navy and Marine Corps. Based on the chassis of a two-and-a-half-ton truck, the DUKW, or "Duck," was a six-wheeled boat-shaped amphibious craft that could carry up to twenty-five soldiers and their equipment from transport ship to shore. Once on shore, the DUKW could navigate virtually any terrain and reach a speed of fifty miles per hour on roads. It was first used in the invasion of Sicily in 1943 but soon found a home with all Allied services in all theaters of operation with modifications made to fit local conditions and needs. Much of the initial training on the DUKW was done at Fort Pierce.

Approximately 270 different kinds of aircraft saw American air service during World War II, ranging from outdated Stearman trainers from the 1930s to experimental jets in 1945. While there is no accurate count of the exact number of these aircraft that were used at Florida bases, included in the mix were commercial aircraft that were adapted for military use. Florida literally became the largest aircraft carrier in the world, and Florida skies were filled with a menagerie of warbirds of every description. How did the Sunshine State achieve this remarkable status?

First, the Sunshine State, which had long depended on tourism as a major part of its economy, had a large number of hotels and resorts available. Following the onslaught of the Great Depression, many of these properties were nearly vacant, as tourism had dried up because of the difficult economic times. Beginning in 1941, the federal government leased more than three hundred hotels in the Miami–Miami Beach area for use as schools for training new officers. From 1941 until 1945, some 100,000 officer cadets passed through these leased venues. They were ideal sites for the military because most of them came with large kitchens and dining rooms, considerable office space, recreation facilities and space for limited medical units. Adjacent beaches and golf courses provided enough open spaces for physical training and close-order drills. New officers and NCOs were essential in providing the leadership for an American military that would rapidly exceed more than 12 million men and women. By placing these once-tourist destinations under military authority, accommodations for recruits were opened rapidly and successfully.

Smaller hotels in other parts of the state were also leased or expropriated to serve as schools for other purposes or as hospitals or as bases for specialized units. The recently constructed Don Cesar Hotel on St. Petersburg Beach was acquired for use as a hospital, while the large Biltmore Hotel in Coral Gables was subjected to a similar conversion. In St. Augustine, Henry Flagler's exclusive hotels—the Ponce de Leon, the Alcazar and the Cordova—were taken over by the U.S. Coast Guard and used as training facilities. So, too, was the historic Belleview Biltmore Hotel, a large wooden resort hotel said to be the largest occupied wooden structure in the world, built by Henry Plant in 1897. The same thing happened to hotels and resorts in Daytona Beach, Hollywood and elsewhere. Even small hotels in small towns were placed under military control. Although tourism in Florida suffered initially from this expropriation of hotels and apartment buildings by the military, it recovered and expanded during the last years of the war.

Just as the military looked for accommodations for its personnel and schools, it also searched for space to house its aircraft and initiate training programs. Once again, the Sunshine State offered an unusually high number of possibilities. During the mid-1930s, many small municipal airports had been upgraded and expanded by workers from the various New Deal programs like the Works Progress Administration and the Public Works Administration. Local governments and civic organizations had spent tremendous amounts of money purchasing large tracts of land for longer runways and needed buildings. Typical of these interactions were those that played out in Melbourne. William Potter, a current member of the governing board of the airport, detailed the growth of the facility from its founding at the very end of the Florida land boom in 1928 through its evolution into an international hub today. In *Melbourne Orlando International Airport: A History from 1928 to 2022*, Potter described the beginnings of the airport in 1928 in a location some six miles from the center of Melbourne. A joint venture between Melbourne and the adjacent city of Eau Gallie, the airport was relocated in 1933 to its current location closer to both cities. In 1940, the two cities entered into an agreement with the Works Progress Administration to acquire additional land and spend $220,000 (more than $4.7 million in today's dollars) in improving and extending runways, constructing hangars and administrative buildings and making other improvements. In 1942, at the urging of city leaders and prominent Florida politicians, the site became the Naval Air Station Melbourne. In 1947, the site was declared surplus by the military and returned, along with improvements, to the city. The story of Melbourne's airport and its subsequent use by the military during World War II was duplicated in multiple cities throughout the state.

By the end of the war in 1945, more than 2.5 million trainees had passed through the Sunshine State. The large number of service men and women who came to Florida for the first time for training would remember their experience favorably, and thousands would return as permanent residents when the war was over.

FLORIDA AND FOREIGN PILOT TRAINING

Florida is very flat with massive swamp land called the Everglades. It was dangerous country and we had special parachute packs in fear of having to make an emergency landing or bale [sic] *out. Snake and alligator infested, a landing there was not to be relished. Huge vehicles called swamp buggies were ready to rescue stranded airmen.*

—Finlay M. MacRae, RAF cadet, Clewiston, 1943

Following the German invasion of Poland on September 1, 1939, Europe was quickly embroiled in a major war, and the United States slowly began preparations for a possible entry into the conflict. With the German conquest of the Low Countries and the surrender of France in 1940, Great Britain found itself alone in fighting the war against Italy and Germany. Because of the difficulties in securing enough aircraft and in finding safe areas for training new pilots, Great Britain transferred its training program to Canada. When these facilities proved inadequate to meet the demand for new pilots, British authorities reached out to the United States for help.

American officials responded by including RAF cadets in the classes of the private aviation companies contracted to train army pilots. Funding for the private training schools for RAF cadets came from the Lend-Lease Act of March 1941. Under the broad terms of this act, the American military had the authority to contract for any item or service considered essential to the security of the nation. The Lend-Lease Act was designed to provide a legalistic cover for the United States and its claim of neutrality, but in reality it was designed to make American arms, ammunition and equipment available to cash-strapped Great Britain, which was facing Germany alone.

It was soon broadened to include China, which was combatting a Japanese invasion and, after June 1940, was extended even further to include Russia. Secretary of War Henry L. Stimson couched his support of the act when he testified before Congress during hearings on the proposed legislation: "We are buying…not lending. We are buying our own security while we prepare. By our delay during the past six years, while Germany was preparing, we find ourselves unprepared and unarmed, facing a thoroughly prepared and armed potential enemy."

In order to maintain the nation's façade of neutrality, British cadets were first transferred to Canada and then shipped south to American schools. Required to wear civilian clothes on their journey, cadets were immediately issued American uniforms and fatigues upon their arrival. "Clad in heavy RAF blue, we got tired and sweaty, but all that was soon to change," wrote Finlay M. MacRae, a cadet assigned to a Florida school at Clewiston. "The very next day we were kitted out in full American clothes and even 4 pairs of lovely light shoes."

The former military bases at Clewiston, Dorr Field and Arcadia were reactivated and leased to the Riddle McKay Aero College, which was open to cadets from Great Britain. The American government supplied clothing, lodging, books, training aircraft and former military instructors. "Although run by the Americans," Finlay MacRae remembered, "there was a core of RAF personnel, mostly administrative. All the flying instructors were American and they varied in age from 20 to 50 years—all highly experienced pilots."

In Lakeland, a school operated by Hal Darr and Albert I. Lodwick opened in 1940 and was contracted by the Army Air Corps to train new pilots, including recruits from Great Britain. By 1943, the Lodwick School had trained more than 1,200 RAF pilots. The same year, Lodwick opened a second school in Avon Park. By the time the Avon Park school closed in 1944, more than 2,800 pilots had gained their wings, most of whom were British. While effective in producing more pilots, these private schools were limited to training fighter pilots who flew single-seat aircraft.

Eventually, six major civilian schools were established for training RAF pilots at bases in Arizona, Oklahoma, California, Texas and Florida. Continuing operations until August 1945, these schools trained a total of 6,921 RAF pilots. In June 1941, Army Air Corps schools were opened to RAF student pilots and graduated approximately four thousand additional pilots. In Miami, American Airways trained more than eight hundred observers and navigators at its facility there. With the increasing importance

Finlay M. MacRae and three other unidentified RAF cadets posing in front of their AT-6 trainer at Carlstrom Field in 1941. *Donna Macrae.*

RAF trainee Finlay M. MacRae took this picture of the sign of Riddle Field at Clewiston, a privately operated base that saw some 1,300 British cadets complete their training. It opened in 1941. *Donna Macrae.*

of carrier-based aircraft in the war, the American navy, at the urging of Aeronautics Bureau chief Admiral John H. Towers, began a program in July 1941 to train British Fleet Arm and RAF pilots on carrier operations, as wireless radio operators and as observers in navy schools. The Towers "scheme" produced some 1,200 British pilots per year.

The primary trainer for the new cadets was the PT-17 or Stearman, a dual-cockpit biplane that was, according to MacRae, "a wonderfully robust machine, fully aerobatic, and safe." Flying was usually done in the mornings, while cadets spent their afternoons at ground school studying such topics as navigation and aerodynamics. In addition to practicing solo flying, cadets were schooled in aerobatics, cross-country flying and formation flying. While the slow and robust Stearman was deemed a "safe" plane for inexperienced pilots, it was not foolproof. Unfortunately, twenty-three RAF cadets were killed while undergoing training. A small cemetery in Clewiston, maintained by the local Rotary Club, is their final resting place.

Upon completion of three months' training in the PT-17, cadets were transferred to the faster and more powerful North American AT-6. Named the "Texan" by the army air forces and the SNJ by the navy, the British referred to it as the "Harvard." Moving from the Stearman trainer to the AT-6 was, in MacRae's words, "similar to moving from a bicycle to a high powered motorcycle, a complete change of speed, thought, and action." With a ceiling of more than twenty thousand feet and powered by a 550-horsepower engine, the AT-6 had a range of 750 miles. Trainees took advantage of the increased range of the AT-6 to undertake long flights to various places. MacRae remembered one such flight, and while his sense of direction might have been wrong, his excitement was undeniable: "We did some long cross-country flights, on one occasion flying North then [West] across the Mississippi [River]—a rare experience. We flew as cadets, one flying, one navigating, turn about."

British cadets (and some of their instructors) had difficulty adjusting to the local culture, particularly in the rural areas of the South. "My advanced instructor came from New York [and] he disliked Florida with its swamps and snakes," MacRae recalled years later. "We were forbidden to drive American cars. The accident rate had been too high so the idea [of driving] was abandoned—we missed the cars and the girls. We were discouraged from seeking lifts in cars driven by black people and it was a serious offence to be caught—sometimes it was unavoidable in Florida." However, "On weekends we headed for Palm Beach, often invited by wealthy families who looked after us very well. I recall a large house with a feature I had never

Finlay M. Macrae, an RAF trainee at Carlstrom Field, would go on to receive the MBE honor and become a noted environmentalist and celebrated piper in his native Scotland. *Donna Macrae.*

seen before or since. The owner pressed a button and the whole side of the room swung out on a central pivot to reveal a well-stocked cocktail bar. Rum and coke was a popular drink in Florida, [but] coke was fairly new to us." Not every weekend was spent associating with the wealthy residents of Palm Beach; cadets sought out other experiences. MacRae fondly recalled, "Some weekends I met up with a fine family who lived by a creek on the edge of the Everglades. There we swam, ate much fried chicken, and enjoyed their warm company. [They were] wonderful, hospitable country folk—[and the wife] became 'my Mama Wadlow.'"

After 1941, the United States extended its various civilian and military programs to include student pilots from various Allied nations. Once again, Florida played host to many of these would-be pilots. In Tallahassee, a civilian contract school was established at Dale Mabry Field in 1938, and in October 1940 work began to expand the airport and bring it under the control of the Army Air Corps as a training base for pilots. The military set a completion date of three months for contractors to increase the number of runways (three) and the size of the base, along with the necessary barracks, administrative buildings, hospital and recreation facilities. Designated the Dale Mabry Army Air Field, the base was formally activated on January 13, 1941, by the Southeast Air District and operated as a primary training base until it was deactivated and returned to civilian control in March 1946.

During the four years of operation, Dale Mabry AAF saw some eight thousand student pilots from Europe and China train at the site. In addition, units of the famed all-Black Tuskegee Airmen received gunnery training at the base prior to their transfer to the European war zones. The nearby Florida State College for Women, now Florida State University, offered trainees courses in math, geography and navigation. Tyndall AAF in Panama City provided training in gunnery and radio communications. More than a dozen student pilots lost their lives in accidents at Dale Mabry and its outlying gunnery range at Alligator Point in Franklin County. The Point was a site shared with Camp Gordon Johnston, an amphibious landing

Chinese Nationalist pilot trainees at Dale Mabry Field in Tallahassee talk with their flight instructor. *Florida Memory.*

training base, in Carrabelle-Lanark, which utilized the beaches for practice landings. A large bullseye, supported by a wooden bunker, was erected on a large sand dune and served as a target for pilots practicing gunnery and skills. In addition to the Alligator Point gunnery range, pilots from Dale Mabry AAF used a 4,480-acre site in Wakulla County for bombing practice. The Sopchoppy Precision Bombing Range was also used by trainees from auxiliary bases in Thomasville, Georgia; Harris Neck, Georgia; Perry, Florida; and Carrabelle, Florida.

Dale Mabry AAF, located just three miles from Tallahassee, employed more than eight hundred civilian men and women from the area and usually had a complement of some four to five thousand military personnel. The base had several runways, barracks for enlisted personnel and student pilots, officers' quarters, a church, a bowling alley, a mess hall, recreational facilities and a hospital. In all, some 133 buildings occupied the nearly 1,800-acre base. Although the field was a military base and closed to general aviation during the war, two airlines, Eastern Airlines and National Airlines, both Florida-based companies, continued to use it for regular flights.

Among the thousands of pilots who received training at Florida bases was a small group of fifty Nationalist Chinese pilots, who were graduates of the Chinese training program created by General Claire Lee Chennault under the auspices of Generalissimo Chiang Kai-shek, the nominal head of the Republic of China. The Nationalist Chinese government was an American ally and, along with the rival Chinese Communist Party controlled by Mao Tse-tung, had been fighting the Japanese since that country had invaded China in 1937. Chennault, an Army Air Corps officer, retired in 1937 and accepted the task of creating and training a capable Chinese air force to counter that of the Japanese army. Using P-66 (Vultee Vanguard) and P-40 (Curtiss Warhawk) fighters supplied by the United States under the Lend-Lease program, Chennault established a training program for Chinese pilots that was virtually identical to that used by the American military. In 1941, a group of fifty was sent to the United States to receive additional combat training.

"General Chennault arranged for us to train all over again at Dale Mabry Army Airfield in Tallahassee, Florida, and at the Arizona Thunderbird aviation school in Phoenix, despite having received trainings on the same courses, with the same aircraft and using the same systems in China," recalled Chenping Ching, one of the pilots in the group. "Naturally, we felt a little insulted and were not happy. To our bemusement, when we reached the base we found out that our American instructor announced to the press that we [were] talented and well-trained pilots, and it seemed like [the] American public was surprised."

Ching had a simple explanation for this: "You see, in the 1940s, the American society was still racially charged. At that time, we learnt that many Americans regarded 'brown men' and 'yellow men' as third-class citizens. Colored people were to sit at the back of buses and at assigned seats in the cinemas. So, General Chennault, with good intentions, wanted to correct the American perceived bias by dispelling the notion that the Chinese were inferior people. We felt shortsighted for thinking he was insulting us earlier on. Needless to say, he earned our respect for his effort. He was a good leader."

Of the original group of fifty Chinese pilots, forty-two successfully completed their training at Dale Mabry AAF and were transferred to the Arizona Thunderbird Aviation School in Phoenix. The civilian-owned Thunderbird school offered an advanced course in combat tactics and aerobatics. The school was unusual because of the large number of Hollywood stars who had invested in the private school. They included

James Stewart (who would later become a B-24 bomber pilot in Europe with twenty successful bombing missions), Hoagy Carmichael, Cary Grant, Henry Fonda, Robert Taylor and Margaret Sullavan. Other notable backers included Hollywood agent Leland Hayward, as well as pilot John Connelly and photographer John Swope, the founders of Southwest Airways.

Chenping Ching returned to China in 1942. He was assigned to the 75th Squadron of the 23rd Fighter Group, the famed Flying Tigers. After the Communist takeover of China in 1949, Ching first went to Taiwan but eventually moved to Hong Kong, where he married and became a merchant. He died in 2022 at the age of 105, a Chinese hero. Although Ching claimed to be the last surviving Flying Tiger, the Chinese government recently feted two American veterans as survivors of the group. Mel McMullen, who is in his late 90s, and Harry Moyer, who is 103, attended ceremonies in Beijing in October 2023.

Although the German military destroyed hundreds of French aircraft following their conquest in 1940, a few French air force units were allowed to operate in Vichy-controlled French colonies in North Africa, and some French pilots managed to fly their planes to the safety of Great Britain before the fall of France. Some of the pilots who made it to Great Britain were enrolled in the RAF, along with pilots from Poland and other conquered nations. Others joined the *Forces Aériennes Françaises Libres*, known by the acronym FAFL, a small, independent air force created by Charles de Gaulle, the head of the French government in exile, and led by Colonel Martial Henri Valin. Initially, the FAFL operated against Vichy French units in Dakar and Gabon without much success.

Following the successful Allied invasion of North Africa in late 1942, French air force units, freed from the control of Vichy France and German supervision, were consolidated into a unified whole and equipped with one thousand Curtiss P-40s. They participated in the Allied air operations against Germany's Africa Corps and the Italian army. Following the defeat of the combined German and Italian forces in North Africa, the FAFL participated in the Allied invasions of Sicily and the Italian peninsula. With new pilots arriving from American training bases and equipped with newer planes, particularly the P-47, the FAFL would also participate in the invasions of France in 1944.

The aircraft operated by the FAFL and the Vichy air units were outdated by the end of 1942, and following the liberation of North Africa, Free French leaders asked for the United States to update their inventory of airplanes and to provide training for new pilots. Major General Carl Spaatz, who commanded the American air forces in Europe, recommended that the student pilots be sent to various training bases in the United States. His recommendation was approved.

The number of aspiring French pilots was reduced by more than 50 percent because they failed to meet basic physical or educational requirements. These individuals were encouraged to receive training in other air-related specialties, and as a result, the French recruits were sent to different bases in the United States. Texas, Alabama, Illinois, Mississippi, Nebraska, Connecticut, Louisiana and Florida training centers received contingents of recruits for training as radio operators, mechanics, bombardiers, navigators and photographers. Some 4,084 French airmen received training between 1943 and 1945. After receiving a basic indoctrination and aircraft familiarization course at Gunter AAF in Selma, Alabama, the French recruits were then assigned to the different bases.

In Florida, the French airmen were dispersed to several different bases. Would-be gunners were sent to Tyndall and Buckingham AAFs, while fifty-eight students in aerial photography courses trained at Pensacola NAS. Student pilots and mechanics were also assigned to Jacksonville Naval Air Station. Wherever they were assigned, according to the website France-Amérique, "the French soldiers integrated into American life. They saved up to buy radios and cars, and dances were organized with students of French from local universities. Several newspapers were even printed in French, including *F-Mail*, *Le Courrier de l'Air*, *Altitude 195* and *L'Escopette*, launched by student gunners stationed at Tyndall Field in Florida."

Jannelle Dupont, writing in the Smithsonian Institute's *Air & Space* magazine in March 2004, detailed the difficulties and the triumphs experienced by American flight instructors in teaching French students the terminology, tactics and philosophy of the U.S. Army Air Forces. Writing about her father Harry Dupont's experience as an instructor at Gunter Field near Montgomery, Alabama, her description could just as easily be about recruits in Florida: "The young recruits received their primary training at…Van de Graaf Field…a field that had been recently carved out of farmland. Civilian instructors conducted primary training through interpreters, including, according to the *Tuscaloosa News*, 'Mrs. Marguerite Taliaferro, a University French teacher, and Mrs. Gerrie Thielens, Tuscaloosa author.' On the flightline, instructors told students what maneuvers they would practice, and the translators did their best to explain the upcoming lesson. *The News* described the process as follows: 'Before flying periods American instructors address Frenchmen on the

A Fighting French mechanic servicing a training aircraft at Jacksonville Naval Air Station, circa 1943. *PICRYL.*

flightline in long slow voices. Interpreters, waiting for convenient pauses, blaze out the same thing in lightning French.'" Dupont continued, "The students, on an average of 22 to 24 years old, lean and blackened by the African sun, listen eagerly, hang on every word."

Urgent calls went out to army air forces personnel seeking individuals with flight experience who could speak French. Ms. Dupont's father had been raised in Louisiana in a Cajun home where French was the primary language. Although different in pronunciation and with a slightly different vocabulary, his Cajun French was enough. To aid other instructors less fluent and to establish a common flying vocabulary for the French students, he put together a glossary and distributed it to students and instructors. Some instructors were assigned to the program because their last name sounded French or because they volunteered. The same scenario was repeated in the navy programs as well.

Ida Emilie Cornwell, along with her sister, Wilna or "Willie," enlisted in the WAVES (Women Accepted for Volunteer Emergency Service) in

This Franco-American program was designed to reinforce the French air force after the Allied landings in North Africa and train five hundred pilots, navigators and mechanics. The results far surpassed expectations, and 4,084 Frenchmen were trained in the United States between 1943 and 1946. The Fighting French are seen here in "V" formation at Jacksonville Naval Air Station. *Florida Memory.*

1943. After completing basic training at Hunter College in New York, she received specialty training in the operation of the Link Trainer system. The Link Trainer, invented by Edwin A. Link in 1931, was a small replica of an airplane with an enclosed cockpit, designed to teach nighttime flying and reliance on instruments. Trainees had access to rudder pedals and a control stick. The cockpit was lit only by a map light and an instrument panel. Students were given a map and a set of coordinates and were expected to use only their navigation skills and instruments to reach the coordinates. The Link Trainer was perched on a flexible metal axle and connected to compressors/generators that could be manipulated by the instructor to duplicate weather conditions, while the student's reactions were plotted on an adjacent map. While not perfect, the Link system was adopted by the military, commercial airlines and private aviation companies as a teaching aid.

After brief tours of duty at naval facilities in Green Cove Springs and Hollywood, Florida, Cornwell was assigned to Jacksonville Naval Air Station and set about performing her duties for students in gunnery school at Cecil Field. Among her students were Free French pilots who had been accepted for training. Language barriers were a concern for her as well, and as she wrote in a letter to her parents on May 28, 1944, "There is a flight of French officers on the base. A few of them can speak English but most of them can't." How did she communicate? "I waved my hands wildly and shoved and pushed the controls like mad. Finally they got the idea." She concluded, "It seems funny that France doesn't send over people who speak English to learn American methods."

The next day, she wrote to her sister, Wilna, who was stationed in San Pedro, California, a more detailed account of her experiences with Free French pilots at Cecial Field: "Today we had a lovely time. We have a flight of Frenchmen on the base. Naturally when choosing men to send over here the French Navy overlooked one small detail of ability to speak English. Did you ever try to teach in sign language? And how do you teach coordination of stick & throttle in 10 simple phrases? The men are all pretty quick to catch on. They didn't know any English when they first arrived. Now they do pretty well."

If Cornwell's experiences as a Link instructor were difficult, they paled when compared to those of the gunnery instructors at Cecil Field. "The gunners really had a time with them. They studied gunnery first & at that time only one of them knew any English. He was supposed to listen to the instructors & then explain to his little friends. There was only one thing wrong with that method. He got fouled up and explained the whole deal backwards." She concluded sarcastically, "Our gunnery instructors were extremely happy."

Ida Emilie Cornwell was transferred to Hawaii in February 1945 and remained there until her discharge from WAVES in September of that year.

The stories of Lieutenant Harry Dupont in Alabama and Ida E. Cornwell in Florida were duplicated at other training bases throughout the States.

Despite initial efforts of the United States to avoid being drawn into World War II, and despite the legalistic maneuvers of American leaders to preserve a façade of neutrality, the reality was that American interests coincided with those of Great Britain and its Commonwealth allies. The United States—through its Lend-Lease Act, the Destroyers for Bases Deal, its coastal patrols in the Atlantic and the Caribbean Sea, as well as many other activities, such as allowing foreign pilot trainees and ground personnel access to bases in the continent—demonstrated its commitment to the defeat of the Axis Powers. The slow movement toward involvement was simply accelerated when Japan attacked Pearl Harbor on December 7, 1941.

Like the coalition that would ultimately defeat the Axis, Florida skies offered a protected haven for a multi-nation amalgamation of pilot trainees.

WARTIME TOURISM AND COMMERCIAL AIR SERVICE

The countryside changed as we moved south and the temperature rose steadily to full summer in Florida. We passed through enormous orange and grapefruit groves. We hadn't seen an orange for years.
—Finlay M. MacRae, British pilot trainee, 1943

For decades, Floridians counted on annual visitors to contribute a significant portion of the state's economy. While their numbers had diminished slightly during the Great Depression, tourists nevertheless added much-needed income for hotel, boardinghouse and resort operators, as well as the hundreds of small mom and pop tourist attractions and fruit stands found along the highways of the state. Florida's participation in several expositions, such as the 1933 Century of Progress and the 1939 World's Fair, had done much to correct the damage done by the Depression.

In 1925, at the height of the land boom, Florida saw more than 2.5 million tourists arrive by train, ship or automobile. Little information is available about airline passengers who came during the 1930s, although numerous photographs of celebrities arriving in the Sunshine State by air were part and parcel of the advertising campaigns of the late 1930s. The collapse of the boom in 1928 also meant a collapse of the tourist industry in the Sunshine State. By 1932, the number of annual visitors had fallen to 500,000, and the loss of revenue prompted the state's political and civic leaders to join forces to try to stimulate this critical portion of the economy. Their solution was to finance, with state and private funds, the creation of a massive exhibit at the Century of Progress fair held in Chicago. Florida's participation was a success, and by the end of 1934, the number of tourists coming to the state had risen to 1.4 million.

The newly created interest in Florida stimulated local entrepreneurs to create new attractions to provide venues for tourists to visit and, most importantly, to spend money. Historian David J. Nelson credits the boost in tourist activities to a state-funded advertising campaign and the various exhibitions. Certainly, state leaders in and out of the government felt some urgency to reestablish this important segment of the state's economy.

During the 1930s, tourists came to the Sunshine State primarily by automobile or railroads. Those who came by automobile tended to explore the less familiar places in Florida, and during the latter part of the decade, a variety of small attractions were added to the tourist offerings—Monkey Jungle, Sunken Gardens, Weeki Wachee Springs and Parrot Jungle were just a few. The automobile allowed visitors to ramble through the countryside informally and freely. Accommodations were usually tourist homes—small operations with two or three rooms—or wayside "motels," aimed at serving automobile travelers with the barest minimum of amenities. For automobile tourists desiring to stay longer, tourist camps, which provided space for trailers and tents and offered such amenities as community showers and bathrooms, were set up by private entrepreneurs and municipal governments. The so-called Tin Can Tourists made up a colorful and reliable segment of annual visitors because they returned year after year.

Those who came by railroad or boat were tied to fixed routes and larger venues. Along these routes, smaller towns like Rockledge and Cocoa offered a mix of good hotels—although not luxurious ones like those in Palm Beach or Miami—and mom and pop operations that could accommodate but a few guests at a time. Tourists who visited these smaller venues tended to stay for longer periods of time than those in larger cities, often returning year after year to the same places and developing family-like ties to the owners and operators.

Even during the height of the Depression, tourism in the Sunshine State did not completely die out. The massive advertising campaigns of the 1930s prevented that, but tourism did not reach the level of that in the mid-1920s. Despite the decrease in tourist numbers, developers continue to erect new hotels, many of which managed to stay in business with a minimum vacancy rate.

With the imposition of rationing of gasoline, tires and other essentials for automobile use following the Japanese attack on Pearl Harbor in December

1941, tourism, which had been recovering during the late 1930s, seemed to be headed in the doldrums. Government monopolization of railroad and ship traffic to transport troops and equipment added to the prospect of no tourism at all, a potentially devastating blow to Florida's depressed economy.

The entry of the United States into World War II and the subsequent takeover of major hotels and resorts in Florida proved to be the salvation for owners in the population centers of the state. In Miami alone, some three hundred hotels and apartment buildings passed into government control. The fees paid to individual and corporate owners ensured the survival of their properties, while improvements made by the military would eventually accrue to them at war's end. By the end of 1942, approximately 85 percent of Miami's hotel rooms, which accounted for one-fourth of the state's total, were leased by the federal government. Eventually, some 500,000 trainees would be housed and schooled in them. Trainees who went through the military schools or who were housed in hotels were well acquainted with the amenities offered by them, and their familiarity would provide a strong basis for postwar clients.

For owners and operators of hotels not brought under the aegis of the miliary, the military's takeover was also a godsend. Wherever servicemen and women trained, families followed. While the military could and did provide housing for officers and permanently stationed enlisted personnel, student transients were largely housed in hastily constructed wooden barracks or tent enclosures that held four to six persons. When families wanted to visit a few days with their loved ones in the service, small hotels and rooming house owners benefited. Not only did the war bring millions of men and women to the state for training, but it also cemented the Sunshine State's role as a leader in the tourism industry.

While historians have focused their attention on the impact of the war on tourism, less attention has been paid to the impact of defense industries on enlarging Florida's permanent population and their equally important role on tourism. During the war, shipbuilding became an important part of the state's contributions to the war effort. Jacksonville, Miami, Tampa and Panama City were home to large shipbuilding yards, which employed from ten thousand to twenty-five thousand workers each. Smaller shipyards on Lake Beresford, Green Cove Springs and Ybor City also employed significant labor forces, while manufacturing plants in smaller towns like Lakeland, Sanford, Brooksville and DeLand produced items ranging from Roebling Alligators to bombs and parachutes. Workers for these operations were recruited from states as far north as

Illinois and as far west as Kansas. Professional labor recruiters competed with military recruiters for warm bodies to fill the ranks of the men and women needed to prosecute the war successfully. Florida's military population grew along with its civilian population.

Finding housing for defense workers and accommodations for friends and family who also came to Florida to visit them proved a daunting task. Following the example set by the federal government, some larger companies contracted with local hotel owners to lease rooms for their workers, while smaller hotel/motel operators advertised available rooms. Trailer parks, tourist camps and rooming house owners benefited from the influx of defense workers. Even individual families supplemented their income by renting spare rooms to defense workers. While the war brought sorrow to some families, for others it meant an end to the Depression.

While the majority of newcomers, civilians and military, came to Florida by train, automobile, bus or boat in the war years, the airline industry, which grew slowly during the early 1930s, experienced a boom in business. As late as 1935, commercial flying had little evolved from the days of stunt flying and novelty flights. On February 27, 1935, the *Fort Lauderdale News* featured an article on the flight operations of William Maycock, the proud owner of a "new four-place Stinson-Reliant," who flew "sight seeing flights and special charter work." According to the article, Maycock, who was at Fogg Field, the city's municipal airport, for only a short time, had flown "41,000 air passengers a distance of 61,000 miles" from July 1 to September 1, 1934. While Maycock might have been proud of his small operation, it was not the model for future success. The number of passengers (four) that could be accommodated at one time limited its profit potential.

The development of new aircraft in the latter part of the 1930s, particularly the Lockheed Electra and the Douglas DC-3, changed the economic picture for commercial airlines. The Douglas DC series embodied these changes from small fabric-covered aircraft to sleek all-metal designs that were faster, larger and more reliable. While statistics on air travel in Florida are scarce until the 1950s, a look at the growth of National Airlines, a Florida-based company, provides some indication about the growth of the industry. Within a decade, National's passenger miles grew an astronomical 436 percent. What happened to National was also what happened to other commercial carriers as airlines gradually replaced trains as a major mode of transportation used by tourists coming to the Sunshine State. Although automobile tourism would continue to dominate for several decades to come, it was only a matter of time before the "Tin Lizzies" would be displaced.

National Airlines made its reputation as an airline by its inclusion of the latest models of aircraft. During the 1930s, National relied on the Lockheed Electra 10E, the same plane flown by Amelia Earhart (shown here) and Fred Noonan on their ill-fated attempt to circumnavigate the globe. *Wikipedia.*

The growth and success of the army and navy aircraft in combat and the development of newer technologies that dramatically improved the safety of military planes had an impact on the general public's acceptance of commercial air travel as an alternative to more traditional modes. The large number of small and large aircraft that saturated Florida skies served to lessen apprehension about flying for civilians, and most accepted flying as something that was no longer reserved for daredevils or the rich but rather was a normal feature of American life.

National Airlines Passenger Growth, 1936–46

Year	*Passenger Miles*
1936	249,799
1938	653,688
1939	1,340,050
1940	3,465,316
1941	7,264,322
1946	108,760,267

Source: American Aviation, *September 1, 1946.*

As money flowed into the American economy from wartime expenditures, commercial air travel moved out of the exclusive realm of the well-to-do to include more and more of the middle class. Because the military operated on a tight schedule, time became an important factor in the move to air travel. Furloughs were short, transfers were quick and weekend passes came and went even more quickly. Friends, spouses and families took advantage of air travel to spend as much time as possible with their loved ones. Commercial air flights reduced the time traditionally spent traveling by automobile, bus or train from days to hours, thus freeing up more time together. There was also the question of convenience to be considered. Rationing continued throughout the war, and securing gasoline or tires for cars could be problematic, while air travel dispensed with rationing issues for individuals. Because commercial air operations were considered essential to the overall war effort, acquiring rationed items proved to be less of a problem for them.

By 1943, Allied success in defeating the Axis Powers was virtually assured. Germany was reeling from defeats in North Africa and Italy, Italian dictator Benito Mussolini had been deposed and a series of naval defeats and successful island invasions had driven the Japanese military into the ever-shrinking borders of the empire. In the United States, success in ending the war was now a question of when, not if.

Tourism, as a separate entity from military assignment or worker relocation, experienced a revival as civilian workers, exhausted from long hours and tight schedules, found themselves flush with cash from good-paying defense jobs and decided that they needed a vacation to relax and rejuvenate. Following the early takeover of hotels and apartments by the military in 1942 and 1943, many venues that had catered to tourists in the 1930s now faced the prospect of empty rooms as more permanent facilities were constructed for the armed forces. The advertising campaigns that featured Florida as a vacation playground, which had been reduced greatly or which had been stopped entirely, were revived. State funding for advertising promotions became available, pressure was put on transportation corporations for increased railroad service and commercial airlines were allowed to share military runways at selected airfields. At Dale Mabry Army Air Field in Tallahassee, for example, National and Eastern Airlines shared facilities with military aircraft. While the airlines could not claim all the credit, local officials reported that seventy-nine thousand visitors had come to the city as a result of the training base there. Consider the overall impact of having almost two hundred military bases in the state.

The renewed effort to reestablish a viable tourist industry paid off, and state officials noted a significant 20 percent increase in out-of-state visitors by the end of 1943. Entertainment venues also reported similar increases in operations, while the amount of money spent on betting reached an all-time high at Florida racetracks. Florida's decision to once again heavily promote the Sunshine State as the ideal vacation getaway during wartime was not without critics, however, but their criticism was largely ignored. Instead of surrendering to their critics, Floridians looked to the wisdom of Henry Ford, who in a 1926 speech argued, "There is, of course, a profound difference between leisure and idleness. Nor must we confound leisure with shiftlessness. Our people are perfectly capable of using to good advantage the time that they have off, after work. That has already been demonstrated to us by our experiments during the last several years. We find that the men come back after a two-day holiday so fresh & keen that they are able to put their minds as well as their hands to work." Vacations, they argued, made sense in sustaining the energy and vitality of America's men and women in the labor force of war industries. Tourism was simply a part of the nation's war effort to create and maintain a high morale.

The fact was that service men and women who trained in the Sunshine State, families and friends who came to see them and tourists who came to relax on vacation were impressed with Florida, and millions returned as permanent residents or tourists in the years after the war. For commercial airlines, their return would prove to be a bonanza.

POSTWAR COMMERCIAL GROWTH

The demand for air travel increased so heavily, however, that on practically all routes it was necessary to make reservations anywhere from several days to several weeks ahead.
—Air Transport Association of America, 1945

Historian William B. Stronge has stated that "the end of World War II brought about a period of readjustment." This readjustment came in several forms. The first was the return to civilian life for millions of soldiers. These soldiers (mostly men but certainly inclusive of women) were forced to readjust their lives. These men and women had served under military command, often for years, and suddenly found themselves back in their prior civilian lives. This readjustment was required not just of discharged service men and women but also their families and communities.

A second readjustment came to the economy. During the war years, the U.S. economy was focused on the war effort. Manufacturers retooled their facilities for production of goods and materials needed to support critical war efforts. With the return of peace, the military complex began the process of disassembly. Military-related corporate earnings fell sharply and quickly. In 1946, military earnings in Florida declined by two-thirds and by a further 50 percent during 1947.

A third readjustment ties with the second. The U.S. economy moved from the wartime rationing and saving, with savings having reached a high of nearly 25 percent of disposable income during the war, to a consumer goods–based economy. Pent-up consumer demand after years of sacrifice resulted in a surge in spending, resulting in a savings decline to roughly 5 percent of disposable income in 1947.

In the postwar years, the population of Florida swelled, rising from approximately 1.9 million in 1940 to just under 5 million in 1960. This rise in population can be attributed to several factors. The first is the returning soldiers. These soldiers accounted for the population increase in two methods. During the war years, more than 170 military establishments were created in Florida. Camp Blanding, located near Starke, became the fourth-largest city in the state, housing more than 55,000 soldiers at a time. Installations at locations such as Key West, Pensacola, Tampa and Jacksonville gave soldiers a look at some of Florida's largest cities. Smaller training facilities located in less populous communities gave soldiers a glimpse of rural Florida and its possibilities. What this amounted to were soldiers who learned of the great weather, scenery and opportunities in Florida. When they returned to the States, many took the opportunity to move south.

The return of peace also led to an increase in births. With families being reunited, the "baby boom" years began. The baby boom generation is traditionally defined as those born between 1946 and 1964, a period with nearly 76 million births nationwide. Home building and owner-occupied homes, a source of considerable wealth for members of the baby boom generation, grew rapidly during the period.

Year	*Florida Population*	*Residents Ages 20–39*	*Owner-Occupied Homes*
1920	968,470	363,477*	94,990
1930	1,468,211	**	153,956
1940	1,897,414	655,622	226,665
1950	2,771,305	864,080	473,124
1960	4,951,560	**	1,047,217

* Ages 20–41 as calculated in census reports.
** Not directly reported.
Source: U.S. Census Bureau

During the postwar years, Florida again became a retirement destination, with retirees seeking to cash out of their northern homes and move to a more hospitable climate where they could take advantage of year-round activities. Between 1950 and 1960, the population of Florida residents over age sixty-five rose by more than 130 percent and accounted for more than 11 percent of the state population. In 1940, native-born Floridians accounted for roughly 50 percent of the state population. By 1960, the number of native-born Floridians in the state had shrunk to around 35 percent.

A return to normalcy, increases in the number and size of families and the growth in senior population with disposable income led to a burgeoning tourism market. Service industries such as hotels/motels, restaurants and roadside attractions saw tremendous growth.

Many tourists were seeking a winter escape from northern climates, while families were often taking advantage of summer breaks, bringing their children to Florida for what they hoped would be a relaxing beach vacation. This diversity of travelers and the split in when vacationers were coming to Florida provided the tourism industry with year-round income.

While many of these vacationers drove or perhaps took a train, air transport was a growing industry and became one that will continue to affect the state of Florida into the foreseeable future.

Nationally and worldwide, air transport was a booming industry in the postwar years. The war showed just how small the world could become, as air travel allowed people to make trips in only hours that previously had taken days. Destinations that once seemed far-flung could now be reached quickly and safely, allowing for additional time at the end destination.

The rise in air passenger travel was immediate after the end of World War II hostilities. Much of this demand was spurred by demand from the army and navy to transport returning soldiers. The Air Transport Association of America (ATAA) reported that during the year 1945, passenger miles increased from 2.26 billion in 1944 to more than 3.5 billion in 1945. During that period, more than 7.5 million passengers flew on the twenty-three domestic and international airlines in the United States. That number is a sharp increase from 1944, when only 4.7 million passengers boarded aircraft. Freight and mail cargo miles increased as well, rising to more than 65-million-ton miles.

The role of women in society had changed rapidly during the war years, with women filling vital roles in all facets of the economy. The ATAA, in a report that is hard to imagine in today's world titled "A Woman's World," reported on ways the airline industry was responding to women and their perceived needs: 62 percent of women surveyed stated that they had plans to fly on a domestic airline with the war being over. The ATAA reported that before the bombing of Pearl Harbor, 20 percent of airline passengers were women, meaning there would be a huge shift in passenger demographics over the next few years.

In its report, the ATAA wrote, "The aircraft of today and tomorrow have many features which appeal particularly to the fair sex." These features included shock mountings to keep noise and vibration to a minimum. Air circulation provided for either cool or warm air to "make flying over the desert or at high altitudes as comfortable as vacationing at the seashore." Large closet space and luggage compartments allowed for easy access to personal items, while at mealtime, a "stewardess" was to attach an individual table to each passenger's chair.

Further, airlines were adding more "stewardesses" to allow for quicker service of meals and take care of other needs. Women were provided with their own lounge, including mirrors, lighting and, in some airlines, fragrant hand lotions.

Designers were hired to update the interior décor of new airplanes. Restful colors such as shades of blue and green were thought to appeal to female travelers, making their journey relaxing and restful. Red tones were thought to stimulate the mind, causing weariness after a flight. Seats were "roomy and luxurious," allowing for women travelers to play cards or hold conversations.

In closing, the ATAA stated, "Yes, from the looks of things to come, it's a woman's world in the air. And more women than ever before will be flying!"

Growth in all areas of aviation was expanding rapidly in the postwar era. In 1941, the number of airline employees nationally stood at twenty-six thousand but had ballooned to fifty-five thousand by the end of 1945 and reached nearly sixty-two thousand in 1947 just two years later. These figures represent not just the frontline pilots and attendants but also include mechanics, hangar and field staff, office and ticketing staff and others. The economic reach of airlines into communities they served was growing rapidly.

Airport construction was occurring nationwide to accommodate demand. At the close of 1946, there were 4,490 airports. Just one year later, there were more than 5,400 airports, an increase of 20 percent. While many of these fields were small, there were nearly 200 runways of at least 5,500 feet in length. By 1950, the country had more than 6,000 runways, with 220 of them containing more than 5,500 feet in length.

The growth in air passenger traffic continued strong in 1947, with revenue passenger traffic increasing almost 8 percent to 13.2 million and revenue passenger miles reaching almost 6.3 billion. To accommodate for this and anticipated future growth, at the close of 1947, airlines had outstanding aircraft orders totaling 263, with companies such as Boeing, Lockheed and Martin receiving the bulk of orders.

By 1950, revenue passenger traffic had increased to 19.3 million, despite the disruption of assisting the U.S. military in mobilizing for war in Korea. At the close of 1950, it was estimated that more than 1,100 aircraft were in scheduled service, a fourfold increase from 1928.

Airlines were continually looking for ways to move passengers safely and quickly. Completion of scheduled mileage was one measuring tool that airlines used. In 1947, airlines completed only 95 percent of their scheduled miles. This record or service not only inconvenienced travelers but also hurt company earnings. Innovations in airline safety were a key factor in increasing operational efficiency.

Several safety measures being implemented included the wider use of an Instrument Landing System (ILS). ILS is a radio navigation system that assists pilots in their runway approach, particularly at night or in poor weather conditions. It was estimated that ILS eliminated more than 55 percent of flight cancelations due to poor weather. Improved runway lighting and technological improvements in communication and air traffic control equipment allowed for further improvements in schedule completion. By 1949, nearly 98 percent of scheduled miles were completed safely.

Flight safety increased during the period due to these technological improvements and an increased emphasis on training and education among employees. In 1945, 76 air transport fatalities were recorded, equaling 2.14 fatalities per 100 million passenger miles. In 1950, there was an increase to 96 fatalities (with only five fatal crashes in 367 million plane miles), but the number per 100 million passenger miles had dropped to 1.2. These numbers were considerably lower than rates for passenger cars, though slightly above rates for bus or passenger trains.

The ultimate measure of success for airlines, however, was profitability. Revenues surged, as would be expected with the increases in revenue passenger miles in the immediate postwar era. The American airline industry, including both domestic and international carriers, produced revenues of $464 million in 1946 but suffered a loss of more than $10 million, evenly divided between domestic and international airlines.

Revenues grew throughout the second half of the decade, reaching a high of $760 million in 1949 before dropping to $589 million in 1950, mostly attributable to the onset of the Korean War and military priorities. As Major General Laurence S. Kuter, commander of the Military Air

Transport Service, stated, "The civil air carriers responded instantly and whole-heartedly to the emergency, and they have done a magnificent job."

Airline net income after taxes showed an unusual but easily explainable trend during the comparable period. After having lost $10 million in 1946, the industry lost a further $26 million in 1947. By the end of the decade, the financials were turning, and in 1949, the industry posted cumulative profits of $19 million and in 1950 a whopping $33.8 million despite the decrease in revenues. The biggest drain on finances earlier in the decade was the need to replace, upgrade and purchase additional aircraft. As the ATAA reported in its 1951 report "Air Transport Facts and Figures," "The domestic fleet was almost completely modernized in the first three postwar years. The cost of this was heavy, and the year 1949 was the first since to see even modest profits for the airline industry as a whole."

An examination of several Florida airports can help provide evidence to the readjustments being made in the state as military priorities faded and air passenger traffic began to dominate.

Miami International Airport is today one of the largest in the country, with more than 50 million domestic and international passengers and nearly 3 million tons of cargo passing through in 2022. More than eighty airlines service Miami to approximately 150 destinations. The economic impact of the airport is estimated at $32 billion annually.

During World War II, the Miami Army Airfield was constructed near the 36th Street Airport. The airfield became a major training center, with an estimated 114,000 men passing through for pilot training. At the war's end, the facility was acquired by the Miami Port Authority, and with considerable foresight, the two airport operations were combined, laying the groundwork for Miami International Airport.

While today more than eighty airlines serve Miami, there are four that played significant roles in the postwar period: Delta Air Lines, Eastern Airlines, National Airlines and Pan American World Airways.

Delta Air Lines, the Atlanta-based powerhouse today, first flew to Miami in December 1945. Flying a small DC-3 that carried only twenty-one passengers, along a route from Chicago with stops in Jacksonville and other points, Delta quickly understood the importance of Miami and relocated 175 employees, creating a new maintenance base for planned expansion of routes. In short order, Delta saw routes expand from Miami to include Knoxville and Cincinnati. During the 1950s, the airline expanded the Miami service to more than seventy cities, including South and Central America routes.

After stints in St. Petersburg and Jacksonville, Eastern Airlines moved its headquarters and maintenance facilities to Miami International Airport. *Smithsonian Institution.*

At the conclusion of the war, Eastern Airlines returned to passenger service, including routes to Miami and Tampa. In 1946, it inaugurated a Miami–San Juan, Puerto Rico route. Eastern was to go on a capital expenditure spree that included an almost doubling in the number of aircraft but also, more importantly to Miami, a $5 million line maintenance building and a forty-thousand-square-foot hangar.

The investments made by Eastern paid dividends, as the airline flew more than 7 million passengers to and from Florida in the decade immediately after World War II. By 1955, Eastern had become the largest industrial employer in the state of Florida.

When the Civil Aeronautics Board granted National Airlines a route from Jacksonville to New York, National gained a seat as a major player in Florida and Miami air traffic. The New York–Miami route was one of the largest and most profitable in the postwar years, and National was now able to fly thousands of passengers on a large portion of that trip. Following this success, National moved its primary maintenance and administrative staff to a new facility in Miami, further positioning them to take advantage of the large passenger base in and out of the city.

National further cemented its position in Miami in 1946 when it began flights to Havana. In the coming years, National was to purchase multiple new aircraft, including eight DC-6, several DC-7 and the Convair 340 and 440 models, which allowed for intermediate distance flights with capacity up to 52 passengers. By 1960, National was operating the DC-8, with seating capacity of around 250, out of Miami on flights to New York City.

After playing a vital role for the United States military during the war, Pan American Airways began the process of converting back to revenue passenger miles. It purchased war surplus planes if appropriate and then converted them for passenger traffic. Most of Pan Am's operations at the time took place at the old 36th Street field part of the airport.

Pan Am was a pioneer in providing a low-cost option for tourists on some flight segments, helping bring the price of air travel within the means of more potential customers. This new option proved successful in luring travelers to its New York–San Juan route. So successful did the idea prove that it soon expanded these offerings to other Caribbean destinations.

With a focus on international travel, Pan Am operations grew steadily in Miami, and unfortunately, it found itself spread to multiple arenas at the airport. Understanding the importance of keeping its Miami presence, it invested heavily in Miami infrastructure around 1960.

Miami International Airport was not the only major airport developing during the postwar time frame. Orlando International Airport is the ninth-largest airport in passenger traffic in the United States and second largest in Florida, with fewer than 500,000 passengers separating it from Miami International Airport. This is an incredible statistic when you realize that the airport was begun in 1942 as Pinecastle Army Airfield, a facility for the U.S. Army Air Corps. The field was reactivated during the Korean War. The field was later renamed McCoy Air Force Base for Colonel Michael Norman Wright McCoy, who was killed in a B-47 Stratojet accident. The property would later become a joint military and civilian facility due to the long runways already in place and the room for future expansion. When McCoy Air Force Base closed, the title to the airfield was returned to the city.

With the opening of Walt Disney World and numerous other family attractions, along with ample meeting and convention locations and the incredible year-round weather, Orlando was poised to explode as an air travel destination. Orlando International Airport received its current moniker in 1976, while retaining the International Air Transport Association code of

MCO. Today, Orlando International Airport and onsite businesses employ more than eighteen thousand people, making it one of the largest employers in the Orlando regional community.

Military investments in other communities laid the groundwork for future expansion of commercial airlines. The small Municipal Airport in Daytona Beach benefited from the navy occupying the field. The navy widened runways and increased the east–west runway to 5,500 feet in length, allowing for larger planes to take off and land safely. In addition, several World War II–era buildings on site have since been used by Embry Riddle Aeronautical University, a major player in pilot training and other aviation activities. Today, Daytona Beach International Airport serves as an attractive alternative to many flyers, rather than the larger and more congested Orlando International Airport.

Drew Army Airfield in Tampa was a large training facility with more than 120,000 combat air crew members passing through its gates. Greatly expanded during the war years, Drew Field was returned to the City of Tampa after the war, with Eastern Air Lines and National Airlines moving their operation from the smaller Peter O. Knight Airport. During the 1950s, international service was first offered by Trans Canada Airlines, and a second terminal was opened to satisfy demand. As air travel surged, Delta, Northeast, Northwest and TWA all began service at Tampa International Airport. Today, Tampa International Airport ranks as the fourth busiest in Florida, trailing Miami, Orlando and Fort Lauderdale–Hollywood.

The post–World War II era proved to be one of considerable growth for the airline industry in the state of Florida. Communities across the state benefited from the military downsizing as airfields, and associated buildings were returned to local ownership. These newly enhanced facilities provided the infrastructure needed to service the growing demand for air travel. With the support and financial assistance of the Florida Department of Aviation, a part of the State Department of Transportation, the Sunshine State enjoys perhaps the most robust support of aviation by any state in the nation.

Not all airfields were returned to local control, however, and as Cold War clouds became more ominous and the threat of war with the Soviet Union a daily concern, airfields such as those in Pensacola, Jacksonville and Key West continued to play a vital role for the U.S. military.

THE COLD WAR, FLORIDA AND OPERATION PEDRO PAN

I remember the fear and concern as we had to practice at school in case of a missile strike. I remember us having to close all the windows in the classroom and then hiding under our desks. It was a scary time for me, as we knew my mother was fearful, so we were too.
—Judy Clifton Steighner

The end of the Second World War meant that the nation was headed back to "normal," and as Spencer F. Wurst noted in his autobiography, *Descending from the Clouds*, "Everyone was clamoring to get the men out of uniform." Wurst and his companions in the 82nd Airborne Division had had enough of war and had seen things most would never discuss again, even with family. Most of the men in Europe had not heard of the atomic bomb until it was dropped and, many felt later, saved them from going to fight in the Pacific. Fighting fanatical Nazis, liberating the horrid death camps of their walking skeletons and seeing the total destruction of many cities along with the unburied dead and wandering, ill-fed populations made a lasting impression on the men and women who served in Europe. Most now wanted nothing better than to return home and quit the endless change of locations brought on by war. As Wurst put it, "I was tired of moving around. I wanted to go home, marry a suitable girl, have a family, and stay in one spot." And that is what he and countless others did, except Wurst was airborne and had the opportunity to fly home instead of taking the slow boats filled with other soldiers and sailors clamoring to reach the safety of our home shores. Flying home was to become something many dreamed about and a lucky few actually experienced.

In Florida, the landscape had changed drastically from the days of the late Depression. During the First World War, the United States built and operated thirty-five flying fields, according to Florida aviation expert Warren J. Brown. The Pensacola Naval Air Station, Curtiss Field and Chapman Field (in Miami) and Carlstrom and Dorr Fields near Arcadia helped produce roughly ten thousand pilots for the air service, as it was called at the time. Most had closed down at the end of that war, but the property remained either owned or leased to the United States. Even before Pearl Harbor, some of these were reactivated, and others soon joined the ranks of operating airports, many funded and built under the Works Progress Administration at the end of the Depression. Many cities had already begun building civilian airports in the late 1930s to help boost tourism and other forms of economic development. As the war clouds built up over Europe, the United States began to streamline its construction of military bases in anticipation of our possible entry into another European conflict. Many of the former functions of the Quartermaster's Corps were transferred to the Army Corps of Engineers, and in Florida that meant the Jacksonville District. Military construction took precedence over the civilian work done under the WPA, CCC and other New Deal operations. As Lieutenant General Brehon B. Somervell argued, "Under no circumstances should the less important, slow moving, civil works be permitted to dominate the reorganization for vital, fast moving and extensive requirements" for the defense effort, noted historian George Buker in his history of the Jacksonville District. Almost overnight, the Jacksonville office saw the civilian staff grow from thirty to more than three hundred, and new assignments rapidly came into their realm, like the expansion of the Orlando Air Base. This meant constructing housing for officers and men (more than two thousand in number), building 8,300 linear feet of dispersal taxiways, new runways, warehouse space of 52,883 square feet and numerous outbuildings for police, firemen and general construction crews. And this was just in the main airbase, which had many satellite branches in Pine Castle, Winter Garden, Mount Dora, Eustis, Umatilla and Apopka. Just to house the more than two thousand men and women to man these stations required an immense effort.

David Colburn, in his essay on "Florida Politics in the Twentieth Century," observed that at the beginning of World War II, Florida had a population of roughly 1.5 million people spread out over the landscape.

The state was still remarkably rural and dedicated to agriculture as the main industry. However, the massive expenditures by the federal government and the migration of 2,122,100 men and women for military training changed everything. The pouring of funds into Florida for airports, harbors, road construction and housing boosted the economic outlook for the state. Tens of thousands of laborers flooded into the state to take care of the needs and services demanded by such an influx of people. As Colburn noted, "The arrival of service personnel, workers and their families led to the dramatic expansion of cities from Miami to Jacksonville to Pensacola and, perhaps as important, provided federal funds to build modern transportation facilities to connect the cities." And, almost in passing, most of the airport facilities used in training our Army Air Corps were, after the war, transferred back to the cities (where the government had taken control under wartime conditions) or given outright as grants to the cities where they were located. Many of these same properties were later to form the basis of our higher education facilities, such as Tallahassee Community College, Florida Atlantic University or Broward Community College, all built in part on former air bases. Others resumed their roles as purveyors of domestic travel and business.

This latter role also involved the state government, which took an active position in promoting the state's resources for the benefit of tourism. The Florida Department of Commerce took a lead in this promotion, and much of what it did has been preserved at the Florida Department of State's photographic collection—much of which is available online. Whether or not the department took pleasure in sending out photographs showing "beautiful young women, scantily clad and lounging around a pool or the ocean, to northern newspapers in the dead of winter" can be questioned, but the impact cannot. More seriously, Governor Millard Caldwell initiated the practice of going on trips to the Northeast and Midwest to promote business. Later administrations took this practice a step further and visited foreign lands hoping to make the Sunshine State a leading destination for tourists and foreign businesses. This effort to make Florida a headquarters for foreign businesses has paid off well and continues to do so. The new population attracted to Florida for business or tourism was not interested in maintaining the "old ways" in politics or in segregating our public facilities or educational institutions. By the 1960s, after Walt Disney changed the face of Orlando and Florida, family tourism became an important element of the state's economy and remains so today. As air travel became more common, so too did its importance in the growth of tourism and the expansion of Florida's economy. Along with air-conditioning and mosquito control, the airplane helped to make modern Florida more amenable to families and businesses.

Getting to Florida was always one of the big questions for those wanting to take advantage of its mild climate and exotic beaches. Geography was an enemy to be conquered, and the growth of the national highway system was only part of the answer. In an age "obsessed with speed and time," the growth of the airlines made the task easier. As Gary Mormino pointedly observed, "World War II had generously endowed Florida with paved runways, modern hangars, and air bases. Cities quickly converted deactivated airports into municipal assets." Quoting the *Tallahassee Democrat* from 1942, which "boldly predicted" that the new era dawning after the war would be different, "It will be the era of the air." And that prediction became the truth. Mormino continued, "Perhaps [the] most important [result was that] the war had welded a bond of trust and faith between Americans and the unnatural act of flying at 20,000 feet inside a fuselage held together by thin layers of aluminum. The pre-1960s Pan Am Sikorsky Clippers and Stratocruisers glamorized flights, combining elegance and air travel, symbolized by the stylish pill-box-hat wearing stewardesses. The trustworthy Douglas DC-3, the 'Gooney Bird,' convinced Americans that air travel was safe." One of the main reasons this statement is important is the fact that this was the one of the first passenger planes to earn a profit for airlines, and with the introduction in 1948 of the "economy class" service, it helped to make air travel affordable for the rising "middle-class" traveler. With the introduction of later, faster models like the DC-7 and DC-8, jet travel, something new in aviation history, brought passengers from New York to Miami in a little over two hours. Jet propulsion would bring another "new era" to flight and, ironically, was first introduced to the world during World War II by the enemy, Germany, and its bevy of talented engineers. These new engines helped Miami become the gateway to South America as one of only two airports (the other was New York) to offer direct flights to Buenos Aires, Caracas and Bogotá.

As an example of the competition between Florida cities for the tourist and business dollar, the history of the rise of Tampa's airport is worth noting. In 1945, Hillsborough County held referendums on the creation of both a port authority and an aviation authority, and each was passed by the voters in the county. Interestingly, Florida's governor appointed the majority of members of both boards, with the mayor of Tampa and one county commissioner serving on each of the boards as well. In 1947, the city purchased Drew

Field from the War Assets Administration, and it immediately changed the name to Tampa International Airport. Two years later, the city deeded Peter O. Knight Airport on Davis Island to the Aviation Authority, thus expanding Tampa International Airport. It was designated an "international airport of entry" and joined Miami and West Palm Beach as a major player in international trade. With the cooperation of the chamber of commerce, the new entity was able to help attract many new businesses to Tampa. Among the other attractions Tampa had to offer were the growing road network that served the city, its long-standing ties to the railroads and the cooperation between private and public businesses in the area. Florida was also touted as a "right-to-work" state, along with Tampa's long history of being anti–organized labor. In 1953, the Aviation Authority approved the expansion of the terminal facilities, as the Federal Civil Aeronautics Board had authorized both National and Eastern Airlines to expand their services to Tampa. Even with this expansion, keynote speaker at the opening Eddie Rickenbacker, president of Eastern Airlines, warned that the new facility was almost already out of date and would need further expansion in the near future. As an indication that Rickenbacker was correct, by 1959 Tampa was being served by seven airlines, not just the three in 1953. In October 1968, the Aviation Authority sold an additional $67 billion in bonds for new construction, and by 1970, an additional bond issue raised $13.5 million, which helped to open the new terminal in April 1971. The improved complex and its growing reputation as a safe and convenient airport also assisted in landing sport enterprises and other new ventures. This also accommodated tourists headed to the newly opened Disney World in Orlando because of the lack of landing facilities in that city.

While tourism and businesses were important to the growth of mid-twentieth-century Florida, military spending continued to be important to the state's economy in the postwar era. Florida's proximity to the Caribbean and South America made it ideal for keeping tabs on potential enemies, real or imagined. In the immediate postwar world, the rapid rise of Communist Russia took the place of the Axis Powers as the focus of American military and diplomatic establishments apprehensive about the expansion of Soviet power. The fear of a Communist takeover had long been a major concern of American foreign policy going back to the infamous "Red Scare" of the 1920s. The United States had even sent troops, along with Great Britain, into the Soviet Union in the years from 1919 to 1921 in support of the pro-Czarist White Russian army, something the young, rising leader Joseph Stalin never forgot. With the aggressive action of the Soviets in establishing pro-

Soviet governments in eastern Europe in the immediate postwar period and occupying these countries, new fears arose. The new American president, Harry Truman, with little experience in foreign affairs, faced the task of dealing with the emerging Soviet threat.

Truman had the blessing of common sense and did not hesitate to rely on many who did have the experience he lacked. Most important of these gentlemen was General George C. Marshall. Marshall himself was the product of an education gently steered by General Fox Conner, who also guided Generals Dwight D. Eisenhower and George Patton. Together, Truman and Marshall developed the policy of "containment," or surrounding the Soviets and their satellites with reliable alliances that could counter almost any aggressive action taken by the new enemy. Truman quickly put the policy in place, and after the Soviets exploded an atomic bomb in 1949, he and his advisors added the concept of "Mutually Assured Destruction," the idea that neither side in an atomic conflict could win a war.

The "balance of terror" was constantly on the minds of many military leaders in the early 1950s, and it did not subside until the 1970s. Truman and his military advisors also faced the dilemma of paring down American armed forces at the end of the war while maintaining enough capability to meet any non-nuclear threat. Truman and his administration had to meet not only the new challenges from the Soviet Union but also emerging threats from China, North Korea and North Vietnam. How does a nation meet such a new threat economically and politically?

Part of the answer was in the creation of the Strategic Air Command (SAC), which had control over all strategic bombers and strategic nuclear forces. Within the purview of this command was the operation of strategic reconnaissance aircraft to identify potential threats. As part of this organization, MacDill Field (later Air Force Base) played a significant role because of its strategic location relative to Latin America and the Caribbean. Commanding this new creation was Major General George C. Kenney, who had been leader of General Douglas MacArthur's air forces during the latter part of World War II in the Pacific. A significant portion of the SAC budget went to the creation and development of high-level reconnaissance aircraft, beginning with the F-2 and other variants of the B-17G Flying Fortress. As early as 1947, some of these craft had been taking photo reconnaissance of the Russian borders, within the twelve-mile limits along international waters (some actually penetrated Soviet airspace, which was duly noted by Stalin and his successors). By the end of 1947,

Patrick AFB in coastal Brevard County was added to the SAC command, which gave more flexibility to the defense of the southeastern United States, while Pinecastle AFB (later renamed McCoy AFB) near Orlando was added to the SAC command in 1951. In 1948, General Kenney was replaced by the former head of the 20th Air Force, Lieutenant General Curtis LeMay, and just a year later, the Soviets tested their first atomic weapon on August 29, 1949. The Joint Chiefs of Staff issued a new strategic plan for SAC command: damage or destroy the Soviets' ability to deliver nuclear weapons, with a secondary objective to protect western Europe from any advances by the Soviets' armed forces. These orders and directives were to be carried out on a steadily reduced budget forced on the military by Congress.

In 1950, the North Koreans invaded the South to create even more confusion and dispersion of force, which put the budget-strapped air force, the leading force in the new "deterrence" concept, on edge. As LeMay noted, "Too many splinters were being whittled off the stick." While all this was taking place, the French suggested the idea of a European Defense Community, separate from the North Atlantic Treaty Organization, the mutual European military pact created in 1949. The French plan, which called for the creation of a pan-European army under a single command,

Postcard showing B-17 bombers flying over Tampa Bay, circa 1942. *Wynne Collection.*

was little more than an attempt to slow down the possible rearmament of Germany that the Truman and Eisenhower administrations desired as a counter to the growing influence of the Soviets in Europe. The United States backed the French plan at first as a means of stabilizing the situation in Europe, but it came to naught when the French General Assembly refused to fund it. The Eisenhower administration responded by sending Secretary of State John F. Dulles to Paris to give the French an ultimatum: allow Germany to rearm and enter into a mutual military pact, such as NATO, or lose American funding for its own rehabilitation. Such funds were critical for France's continuation of its colonial war in Indochina, for which the United States was already paying nearly 75 percent of the costs. The French had no other option but to accept the rearmament of its enemy.

The United States quickly created a new SAC-controlled air force, the 16th, and stationed most of its B-47 Stratojet forces in North Africa, Spain and Turkey. B-47 were medium-range bombers that traded speed for distance and could be rapidly deployed when needed. SAC also moved to put a portion of its main bomber force on full twenty-four-hour alert status, including the aerial refueling aircraft. It was a very tense time for the air force, SAC and the nation. This also meant that both MacDill and Patrick AFB would be included in the alert status and standing as the force went into a defensive mode in the Americas as the Cold War became more intense. The United States and its NATO allies were determined to remain resolute in the face of the Soviet efforts to find weaknesses.

The ultimate test came with the attempt to arm Cuba with Soviet missiles that could easily reach many bases in the United States, including Florida, in October 1962. By 1953, the Soviet Union had successfully exploded both atomic and hydrogen bombs but initially lacked the means of effectively delivering them to targets outside its borders. Soviet advances in missile technology and aviation throughout the 1950s matched those made by the United States, and both nations poured resources into the creation of intercontinental ballistic missiles capable of reaching each other if the Cold War turned into a physical conflict. The Soviets' successful launch of the first satellite, *Sputnik*, in 1957 had taken the Americans by surprise and added to the instability of the relations between the two nations. Although the United States quickly followed with its own satellite launch, the Soviet success revealed a glaring deficit in America's defense network. What was lacking at this time was more accurate reconnaissance of the Soviet Union and its allies to ensure that such surprises did not take place again.

The failure of American intelligence agencies to successfully monitor the progress of Soviet missile technology caused the United States to develop the long-range, high-altitude U-2 aircraft, which could fly over the Soviet Union and photograph suspected military installations. Although the military thought the U-2 to be beyond the range of existing ballistic missiles and Russian planes, a U-2 piloted by Francis Gary Powers, a civilian pilot employed by the Central Intelligence Agency, was shot down by a missile on May 1, 1960. Although President Dwight D. Eisenhower denied any connection to the incident, Powers, who survived the shootdown, was put on trial and convicted of spying. American-Soviet relations reached an all-time low, and the world watched anxiously, fearing that the Cold War would erupt into a real war.

Stung by the Russian success at shooting down the U-2 spy plane, the Eisenhower administration—with the full cooperation of the CIA, the U.S. Air Force and NASA—placed a new emphasis on the development and use of the CORONA KH series of photographic satellites, which could monitor Soviet military activities from the safety of outer space. Sophisticated photographic analysis identified established bases, newly constructed bases, missile sites and military movements.

With the world on the brink of war, tensions between the Soviet bloc and the United States remained high.

Operation Pedro Pan

During the tense years following the revolution that brought Fidel Castro to power, there were many attempts to remove or free Cubans who wanted to leave and bring them to the United States. Pan Am had a long history of flights in and out of Cuba, and during pre-Castro Cuba, the airline flew up to fourteen flights each day between the United States and Havana, with Miami being the busiest airport taking in these flights. Between 1960 and the Cuban Missile Crisis of October 1962, a clandestine airlift of Cuban children, now known as Operation Pedro Pan, took out a total of 14,048 children and brought them to the United States, most unaccompanied by their parents or other family members. Working with the Catholic Church and other denominations, these children received visas and assistance to come to freedom. Pan Am and KLM were the two most important private airlines working with the churches and private organizations.

These children left families and friends behind to come to a new country where the language and customs were new and unfamiliar. As one young gentleman noted in his memoirs, "[A]t the age of fifteen, I was separated from my mother—in fact—my whole family and from everything else I knew....Leaving Cuba was a wrenching decision but one that my family and I had determined to be our only option," according to former United States senator from Florida Melvin Martinez, quoted in Charlie Imbriani's *Pan American Airways: Missions of Mercy and Evacuation Flights*.

Pan Am also was the airline most responsible for hauling the prisoners of the failed Bay of Pigs fiasco back to the United States once the negotiations were completed between parties in the United States, primarily the Families Committee and others and the Cuban authorities of Castro's government. The first 60 men were released, injured and wounded, on April 14, 1962, and these members of Brigade 2506 arrived in Miami from José Martí Airport on that date; that left 1,113 men behind. Castro wanted tractors, medicine, surgical equipment and baby formula in exchange for the men and an additional $2.9 million in "indemnity" for the first 60 sent back earlier. Many of the medicines were donated by Merck and Warner Lambert, and nearly two hundred American companies donated more than $53 million in other needed equipment and baby food. All of this was hauled to Miami and shipped to Cuba aboard Pan Am flights, which were manned by volunteers. Much of the materials were transported on three freighters and two passenger planes at Christmastime 1962, to meet the promise that the remainder of the brigade would be home by Christmas. Some of the remaining funds were raised by Cardinal Cushing and others connected to the Catholic Church and other denominations. Most of the arrangements were made through the American Red Cross. In total, some thirty-five flights passed between Miami and Cuba to get the goods to Cuba and the men back to the United States. No data currently exists that details how much these flights cost Pan Am, but it was substantial—a remarkable achievement by one of the premier airlines of its day.

These tensions continued to escalate following the election of John F. Kennedy in 1960, although the focal point shifted from Europe to Cuba. Following his overthrow of the regime of Fulgencio Batista in 1959, the revolutionary leader Fidel Castro created a Marxist state to replace the dictatorship of Batista. American business leaders, crime syndicates and Cuban expatriates facing the loss of property and positions put pressure on the American government to overthrow Castro. In April 1961, the ill-fated Bay of Pigs invasion was launched by Cuban volunteers and quickly suppressed by the Castro regime. The failure of this invasion set the stage for another confrontation between the United States and the Soviet Union—one that brought the Sunshine State to center stage of American foreign policy and a potential world war.

Following the aborted Bay of Pigs invasion, Cuba looked for allies that would provide some protection against any further attempts by the United States and its surrogates to oust the Castro government, and it found a willing partner in the Soviet Union. In October 1962, a CIA analyst, David Doyle, spotted newly constructed medium-range missile sites in Cuba that were identical to those previously identified in the Soviet Union from CORONA photographs. Subsequent U-2 overflights and naval reconnaissance flights confirmed the sites and identified them as being typical of Soviet sites photographed earlier over the Soviet Union. The Kennedy administration immediately put the Soviet Union on notice that the missiles were to be removed or the United States would forcibly remove them or destroy them through aerial attacks.

For twelve long days, October 16–28, the world watched with bated breath as the Soviet Union and the United States deployed aircraft, ships and submarines around the island nation and hurled threats and ultimatums at each other. President Kennedy warned the citizens of the United States and the rest of the world of the danger Soviet missiles in Cuba posed in an October 22, 1962 speech: "This urgent transformation of Cuba into an important strategic base—by the presence of these large, long-range, and clearly offensive weapons of sudden mass destruction—constitutes an explicit threat to the peace and security of all the Americas, in flagrant and deliberate defiance of the Rio Pact of 1947, the traditions of this nation and hemisphere, the joint Resolution of the 87th Congress, the Charter of the United Nations and my own public warnings to the Soviets of September 4 and 13."

The Cuban Missile Crisis put Florida in the front row of the Cold War. As the United States prepared for a possible invasion of Cuba or a possible nuclear missile strike, thousands of troops were shipped to Florida, missile batteries were set up in the Everglades and along the beaches of the Sunshine State and entire fighter and bomber air wings were transferred to MacDill, Homestead and Patrick Air Force Bases. An around-the-clock naval blockade was established that completely surrounded Cuba, denying shipments to and from the island nation. Civilians were urged to prepare for a possible nuclear attack, and schoolchildren practiced "duck and cover" drills daily. For older Floridians, it was *déjà vu*, recalling the clamor that followed the Japanese attack on Pearl Harbor in 1941.

A diplomatic solution was worked out that averted war, and the Soviet Union agreed to remove its missiles and bases from Cuba, while the United States removed some of its missiles from Turkey. Aircraft from Florida bases continuously monitored the removal process, while the American military remained on the alert for possible trickery or a surprise attack. For those twelve days in October 1962, the clear skies of the Sunshine State provided the stage for the most dramatic confrontation between the world's superpowers as they inched toward the edge of Armageddon.

THE RACE FOR SPACE

We choose to go to the moon in this decade and do the other things, not because they are easy, but because they are hard.
—John F. Kennedy at Rice University, September 12, 1962

Man dreamed of space flight for years before it became reality. In 1938, Flash Gordon, portrayed by Buster Crabbe, took a trip to Mars to fight two old enemies, Ming the Merciless and Azura, the Witch Queen of Mars, in the theatrical release *Flash Gordon's Trip to Mars*. Later that same year, Orson Welles's radio adaptation of H.G. Wells novel *The War of the Worlds* caused a brief panic when many listeners thought that the Martian invasion was true.

Writers such as Philip K. Dick, Isaac Asimov, Arthur C. Clarke, Theodore Sturgeon and others used space as a setting for their science-fiction works. Pulp magazines and comic books such as *Galaxy Science Fiction*, *Space Stories*, *The Magazine of Science Fiction and Fantasy*, *Journey into Unknown Worlds* and dozens of others allowed readers, often boys, to escape their reality with dreams of fighting evil and often winning the girl.

In the days before and at the start of true space exploration, television shows were beginning to regularly incorporate the theme of space travel. *Star Trek*, *Lost in Space*, *Tom Corbett, Space Cadet* and *The Twilight Zone* helped viewers envision what a world in the stars might be like. Hanna-Barbera Productions was not to be left behind, and with *The Jetsons*, children were able to dream of flying cars, robot maids, large screens where your boss pops up like magic and schools with names such as Little Dipper School.

America's first rocket launch from Cape Canaveral was the Bumper Eight, a captured German V-2 rocket, from Launch Complex Three on July 24, 1950. *PICRYL.*

In the real world, the race for space was a key component of the Cold War, the political standoff that took place between the United States and the Soviet Union in the years after World War II. Both sides threatened, attempted to bully and used propaganda and fear in their efforts. The game of one-upmanship in the battle for dominance in space was a leading characteristic of American and Soviet leadership.

In an exaggerated sense, the race for space can be traced to the discovery of the Florida peninsula by the Spanish in the early 1500s. In a 1992 exhibit, the Smithsonian Institution stated that the name Cape Canaveral roughly translates to "place of the cane bearers" and was named by the explorer Francisco Gordillo, after he was shot with a cane arrow by the Ais people inhabiting the area. Historian William Barnaby Faherty states that the name Canaveral came from early Spanish sailors who, when traveling north along the Florida coast, spotted an abundance of cane reeds. No matter the exact origin, the name Cape Canaveral has been accepted for five hundred years.

General view of the exterior of the Vehicle Assembly Building (VAB) at the Kennedy Space Center. The view is of the two solid rocket boosters stacked and assembled on the Mobile Launch Platform (MLP) passing through the sliding doors of the VAB. Note in the approximate lower quarter of the image, toward the right-hand side, on the MLP, there is a person standing to give a sense of scale. *Library of Congress.*

Cape Canaveral, the land area most associated with NASA and rocket launches, is a rather small barrier island about ten miles wide at its widest and thirty-four miles north to south. The John F. Kennedy Space Center occupies more than half of the Cape, while the Cape itself is located within the boundaries of the Merritt Island National Wildlife Refuge. The refuge is more than two hundred square miles, encompassing fragile ecosystems that serve as home to more than one thousand plant species and more than five hundred wildlife species, including those in threatened and endangered status such as the west Indian manatee, several species of sea turtle, the Florida scrub jay and southern bald eagle.

The "red scare" truly came alive on October 4, 1957, when the Soviet Union launched *Sputnik I*, the first man-made satellite successfully launched into the low Earth orbit. *Sputnik*, a Russian term for satellite, reached a top speed of about eighteen thousand miles per hour and stayed in orbit until January 4, 1958, when it fell into Earth's atmosphere and burned up upon reentry after nearly 1,500 orbits around the planet.

The United States was not far behind, launching *Explorer 1* on January 31, 1958. Under the skillful leadership of Senate Majority Leader Lyndon B. Johnson, the Aeronautics and Space Act was shepherded through Congress in 1958, and on October 1, President Dwight D. Eisenhower signed the bill, establishing the National Aeronautics and Space Administration, or NASA. All non-military space activities were then placed under the umbrella of NASA.

Space travel has evolved at a speed nobody in the early days of NASA could have imagined. Less than one week after the formal creation of NASA, Project Mercury was announced. Mercury had as its goal to put a human on the Moon. The first team of astronauts was announced in April 1959 and included Scott Carpenter, Gordon Cooper, John Glenn, Gus Grissom, Walter Schirra, Alan Shepard and Donald Slayton.

The race to put a man into space was heating up, and on April 12, 1961, the Soviets launched the *Vostok I* with cosmonaut Yuri Gagarin aboard. Gagarin completed one orbit of Earth, with the *Vostok* staying close to the edge of the upper Earth's atmosphere at approximately ninety-one nautical miles. Gagarin's flight lasted only 108 minutes before he exited the capsule and safely parachuted to earth.

Only days later, on May 5, 1961, NASA launched astronaut Alan Shepard on a fifteen-minute suborbital flight aboard the *Freedom 7*. It would be almost a full year until John Glenn made three orbits of the planet on February 20, 1962, aboard the *Friendship 7*.

On February 10, 1960, President Dwight D. Eisenhower visited Cape Canaveral to witness the progress of America's rocketry program in the aftermath of Russia's successful launches of *Sputnik I* and *Sputnik II*. Photograph by Warren K. Leffler. *Library of Congress.*

President John F. Kennedy became a lead proponent of NASA and space exploration. In one of his most famous speeches, to a joint session of Congress on May 25, 1961, Kennedy pronounced:

> *I believe that this nation should commit itself to achieving the goal, before this decade is out, of landing a man on the Moon and returning him safely to the earth. No single space project in this period will be more impressive to mankind, or more important for the long-range exploration of space; and none will be so difficult or expensive to accomplish. We propose to accelerate the development of the appropriate lunar space craft. We propose to develop alternate liquid and solid fuel boosters, much larger than any now being developed, until certain which is superior. We propose additional funds for other engine development and for unmanned explorations—explorations which are particularly important for one purpose which this nation will never overlook: the survival of the man who first makes this daring flight. But in a very real sense, it will not be one man going to the Moon—if we make this judgment affirmatively, it will be an entire nation. For all of us must work to put him there.*

Additional Mercury flights were undertaken by astronauts Scott Carpenter and Walter Schirra, and finally, the last Mercury flight was taken by Gordon Cooper on May 15, 1963. Cooper completed twenty-two orbits of Earth.

While the Mercury program did not provide for an American to be the first human in space, nor did it complete the most orbits of the planet, it did prove to the public, Congress and President Kennedy that NASA had the ability to move forward and achieve further gains. Programs such as Gemini, Apollo and the Space Shuttle were built on the success of Mercury.

On November 22, 1963, John F. Kennedy was assassinated in Dallas, Texas, while riding in a motor parade. As a chief backer of NASA and the space program, the newly sworn in president, Lyndon B. Johnson, vowed to continue Kennedy's space-oriented goals.

In the days immediately after the assassination of President Kennedy, Johnson took to the nation's airwaves, announcing an executive order renaming the launch facility and Cape Canaveral itself in honor of the fallen president. Unfortunately, this name change did not sit well with local residents, who didn't care for such federal intrusion in their daily lives, and the city of Cape Canaveral and Port Canaveral maintained their names.

The name Canaveral also held historical importance, harkening back to the Spanish landing in Florida more than four hundred years prior, and in 1973, at the direction of the Florida legislature and Governor Reubin Askew, the name Canaveral was returned to official Florida documents. Later that year, the U.S. Board of Geographic Names agreed, and the name Cape Canaveral was returned at the national level.

NASA continued toward its goal of putting a man on the Moon, and after multiple failed missions, the Ranger program proved successful in photographing the surface of the Moon. In total, nearly twenty thousand images provided scientists with an up-close view of the crater-pocked surface of the Moon. Building on its string of success, NASA continued forward with the Gemini project, the preparatory work for launching man to the Moon. The Gemini spacecraft were designed for two persons with a longer flight duration capability. During the period of March 1965 through November 1966, ten Gemini missions orbited Earth, with the longest flight lasting fourteen days.

One of the highlights of the Gemini program was *Gemini 4*. While Russian cosmonaut Alexi Leonov, of the *Voskhod 2*, became the first person to leave a space capsule and return safely on March 18, 1965, the United States was not far behind. Flying aboard *Gemini 4*, less than three months later, American astronaut Ed White successfully floated (walked) in space for twenty minutes, traveling at a speed of seventeen thousand miles per hour.

Mercury and Gemini were successes of the highest order. The monetary cost was high, but the United States was proving that it would not be intimidated or left behind by the Soviet Union in the race for space. The next missions would be those of the Apollo. Huge successes and tragic failure would await NASA in the following years.

As described by NASA, "Apollo was a three-part spacecraft: the command module (CM), the crew's quarters and flight control section; the service module (SM) for the propulsion and spacecraft support systems (when together, the two modules are called CSM); and the lunar module (LM), to take two of the crew to the lunar surface, support them on the Moon, and return them to the CSM in lunar orbit."

Apollo 1, originally designated Apollo-204, was scheduled for launch on February 21, 1967. Its goal was to be the first low orbit launch of the command and service modules in anticipation of future manned launches to the lunar surface. Three experienced astronauts were chosen for the honor of flying on *Apollo 1*: Gus Grissom, Ed White and Roger Chaffee.

The three astronauts boarded the *Apollo 1*, on launch pad 34, at 1:00 p.m. on January 27, 1967, in preparation for testing a launch rehearsal.

While some technicians did have concerns about the test, overall, engineers considered the test safe as no fuel was loaded in the craft.

After the astronauts were strapped in and connected to the oxygen and communication systems, Grissom noticed a peculiar smell, "buttermilk" being how he described it. The launch trial countdown was paused to investigate. The smell proved temporary, and the countdown started again.

Enclosing the astronauts in the module was a three-hatch system, an inner hatch and two outer hatches, to act as heat shields and protective covering. Once the hatches were closed, the cabin was filled with pure oxygen at a level higher than atmospheric pressure. By now, the time was 6:30 p.m. At 6:31 p.m. one of the astronauts, believed to have been Gus Grissom, is heard yelling, "Hey! Fire!" Seconds later, a different astronaut can be heard saying, "We've got a fire in the cockpit." The astronauts and outside crew worked furiously to open the hatches, with no success. After more than five minutes, outside crews were able to open the three hatches, but it was much too late for the three men inside. Autopsy results determined that the men died due to the high levels of carbon monoxide in the capsule. Third-degree burns were found on all three men, but reports stated that these occurred after death.

Investigations into the tragedy determined five major causes. The first being "vulnerable wiring carrying spacecraft power." The second cause was the pure oxygen in the capsule at higher than atmospheric pressure. A third cause was stated to be the inability to remove the hatches when at high pressure. Fourth, the cabin was determined to have contained an extensive distribution of combustible materials. Finally, there was a lack of adequate emergency preparedness.

Despite the tragedy and loss of three talented astronauts, the Apollo program continued. NASA still had the political support it needed, and the agency retained the support of astronauts in the program. Although the Apollo program was grounded for twenty months to allow for investigation of the tragedy and a redesign of the capsule to try to prevent further accidents, unmanned launches continued. The goal of putting a man on the Moon remained in place.

The Apollo program roared back to life in 1968. On October 11, 1968, *Apollo 7*, carrying Walter Cunningham, Don Eisele and Walter Shirra, powered into orbit courtesy of a modified version of the powerful Saturn V rocket. Only two months later, on December 21, *Apollo 8* took flight with William Anders, Frank Borman and James Lovell aboard. *Apollo 8* completed ten lunar orbits before returning the astronauts safely to Earth on December 27. NASA had received its Christmas gift in the form of safe launches and returns.

The following year started off well with successful flights on *Apollo 9* and *10*. It would be *Apollo 11*, however, that became perhaps the most famous of all spacecraft. Early in the morning of July 16, 1969, astronauts Neil Armstrong, Buzz Aldrin and Michael Collins boarded *Apollo 11*, powered by a Saturn V rocket, with the goal of achieving Kennedy's 1961 goal of putting a person on the Moon. At 9:32 EDT, *Apollo 11* was launched, propelling NASA to a level of success unimagined just years prior.

After entering lunar orbit on July 19, Armstrong and Aldrin boarded the Lunar Module *Eagle* to prepare for a Moon landing. Collins stayed in the Command Module, piloting the *Columbia* safely in lunar orbit in preparation for the return of Armstrong and Aldrin and their return to Earth. On July 20, more than six hours after landing on the lunar surface, the *Eagle*'s hatch was opened and Neil Armstrong emerged. Safely on the lunar surface, Armstrong uttered the famous words: "That's one small step for [a] man, one giant leap for mankind."

Aldrin was to follow. Together, he and Armstrong would plant the flag of the United States on the surface, talk live with President Richard M. Nixon and collect more than forty-seven pounds of material to bring back to Earth. After completing their mission, Armstrong and Aldrin piloted the *Eagle* to rendezvous with Collins and the *Columbia*. On July 21, the three astronauts were reunited after a successful mission.

Columbia splashed down in the Pacific Ocean on July 24, and a large rescue team in the vicinity assisted the returning astronauts to safety. Because of the unknown conditions the astronauts had encountered, they were placed in a twenty-one-day quarantine.

Deemed safe and their quarantine lifted, the astronauts participated in ticker-tape parades in Chicago and New York City. The three men were presented with the Presidential Medal of Freedom from President Nixon. They would later go on a tour of the world, stopping in twenty-two countries, where they met with leaders and dignitaries. The Apollo program would continue for three more years, culminating with the final manned mission, *Apollo 17* in December 1972. In total, the Apollo program would put twelve men on the Moon over six lunar landings.

More than fifty years after their incredible achievement, *Apollo 11* and its astronauts Neil Armstrong, Buzz Aldrin and Michael Collins are still spoken of with reverence. Their achievements are still a point of American pride and an inspiration to the astronauts of tomorrow who hope to build on this legacy and go further, both literally and figuratively.

With the ending of the Apollo program, NASA moved ahead with its Space Transportation System (STS) program, known as the Space Shuttle. The Shuttle program would bring some of the highest highs and lowest of lows to NASA over a nearly forty-year existence.

The basic design of the Shuttle seems simple, particularly considering where space flight has advanced to in the years since. The Shuttle consisted of a reusable orbiter that had capacity for up to eight people. The orbiter was powered by a disposable external fuel tank and two reusable solid rocket boosters. At the completion of a mission, the orbiter would land, much like an airplane, at Edwards Air Force Base in California or Kennedy Space Center in Florida.

Margaret Weitekamp, of the Smithsonian Institution's Air and Space Museum, in writing for the *Florida Historical Quarterly*, stated that there were "hopes in the early 1980s that this regularly operating spacecraft were the beginning of an everyday space age."

In total, NASA operated five Shuttles: *Atlantis*, *Challenger*, *Columbia*, *Discovery* and *Endeavour*. The program initiated 135 launches and returned 133 safely to earth. The program flew 833 crew members, 14 of whom perished in two separate accidents. A total of 355 individual astronauts flew Shuttle missions, including 306 men and 49 women. Some of the goals of the Shuttle program included cycling astronauts in and out of the International Space Station (ISS), providing equipment to and returning equipment from the ISS, servicing the Hubble Telescope and launching satellites. Shuttle astronauts regularly performed experiments, advancing the understanding of weightlessness.

The Shuttle program was able to trace its roots to 1972 in the post Apollo and Skylab years. The first test program, begun in 1977, was undertaken by *Enterprise*, providing information on flight systems, ferrying a Shuttle on a larger transport plane and landings. Tests were run under differing circumstances, allowing NASA to gather as much information as possible. In total, sixteen Approach and Landing Tests (ALT) prototype flights were performed.

April 12, 1981, marked a new day in the history of space flight as STS1, *Columbia*, became the first manned Space Shuttle launch, taking astronauts John Young and Robert Crippen to space for a period of just over two days. This marked Young's fifth trip to space, having earlier flown on *Gemini 3* and *10* and *Apollo 10* and *16*. He walked on the Moon during the *Apollo 16* flight. The two-member crew spent slightly over fifty-four hours in space.

The highlights of the flight included running many experiments and tests. Young and Crippen received a call from Vice President George H.W. Bush congratulating them on their mission. President Ronald Reagan was unavailable because of an assassination attempt two weeks prior. Perhaps the greatest and most lasting accomplishment was successfully and safely landing the Shuttle at Edwards Air Force Base, proving that reusable launches were possible.

Over the following year and a half, *Columbia* would make four more missions before the introduction of *Challenger* to the Shuttle fleet in April 1983.

During STS-6, the first flight of *Challenger*, astronauts Paul J. Weitz, Karol J. Bobko, Story Musgrave and Donald H. Peterson successfully completed a trip of five days, safely landing at Edwards Air Force Base. During their mission, the crew completed the first extravehicular activity, as Musgrave and Peterson spent more than four hours performing tests in the payload bay. In addition, the crew successfully deployed the first Tracking and Data Relay Satellite. *Challenger* would fly two additional successful missions during 1983.

August 1984 saw the introduction of a third Shuttle, the *Discovery*. Later in 1984, *Challenger* astronauts made history when during an October 5 through October 13 mission, several firsts were accomplished. STS-13 saw the first mission to include two women astronauts on the same flight as Mission Specialists Kathryn D. Sullivan and Sally K. Ride played crucial roles in the success of the flight. On October 11, Sullivan became the first woman to walk in space when she and Mission Specialist David C. Leestma spent three hours outside the Shuttle performing tests on the Orbital Refueling System. During the flight, Payload Specialist Marc Garneau became the first Canadian in space. STS-13 traveled slightly under 3.3 million miles and completed 133 orbits of Earth during its flight. *Challenger* became only the second Shuttle mission to land at Kennedy Space Center, saving NASA time and money in preparing it for the next mission in April 1985.

The Shuttle *Atlantis* joined the program with a maiden flight on October 3, 1985. Lasting just over four days, the mission included five astronauts who successfully launched U.S. Department of Defense satellites into orbit. During this mission, Commander Karol J. Bobko became the first astronaut to fly in three different shuttles, including two maiden voyages.

Confidence in the Shuttle program was running high at NASA, in the federal government and among U.S. citizens. Manned launches were a regular occurrence. In 1985, nine successful Shuttle missions were launched, using three different vehicles. A banner year was anticipated in 1986.

When Space Shuttle *Columbia*, STS-61-C, lifted off from Kennedy Space Center on January 12, 1986, seven crew members were aboard, including the first Costa Rican–born astronaut, Franklin Chang-Díaz; Charles Bolden, the second African American shuttle pilot; two future NASA administrators; and sitting U.S. House member Bill Nelson. In a whirlwind six-day mission, shuttle astronauts deployed a major communications satellite and performed multiple experiments, including those on microgravity, seed germination and the effects of space on artwork. Bad weather plagued landing attempts, extending the flight by two days and forcing a California landing. Despite this comparatively minor setback, the mission was deemed a success.

A successful year was beckoning as the Space Shuttle *Challenger* was rolled to the launch pad for its tenth mission to space, following quickly on the heels of the successful *Columbia* mission. The mission carried seven astronauts, including Christa McAuliffe, the first teacher to fly in space, having been

Mobile Launcher One and Vehicle Assembly Building at Cape Canaveral Space Center near Titusville, Florida. *Library of Congress.*

selected from more than eleven thousand applicants, as a part of the NASA Teacher in Space Project (TISP).

The Teacher in Space Project was first announced by then president Ronald Reagan in 1984. The goal of the program was to honor schoolteachers while inspiring their students. The overarching aim was to inspire young students in the study of what we now call STEM (science, technology, engineering and mathematics). TISP was not founded to create professional astronauts; rather, the selected men and women would perform as payload specialists, including teaching a lesson from space, and then return to their classroom duties, providing new insights to the students and districts.

The morning of January 28 was unusually cold for Florida. Overnight forecasts had called for temperatures to drop to eighteen degrees Fahrenheit, a number seldom seen even in northern Florida. Concerns over the cold and its effect on rubber O-rings on the Shuttle were discussed by the Shuttle manufacturer, NASA engineers and NASA administrators. As the morning drew on, temperatures slowly climbed and ice on the Shuttle melted, alleviating some concerns. At 11:38 a.m. EST, local temperatures had reached a still cold thirty-six degrees, and the *Challenger* and crew were given the go ahead for launch.

While the launch was anticipated to go off as had dozens prior, upon liftoff smoke was witnessed from the right solid rocket booster (SRB). Abnormally low temperatures had prevented O-rings from forming their required seal, allowing gases to escape, further damaging the delicate, yet essential, rings.

At fifty-eight seconds into flight, a plume of smoke was seen from the right SRB as high winds and aerodynamic forces converged on the Shuttle. Forces beyond the control of ground crews or astronauts were taking over. This hard science discussion is beyond the scope of a general history, however.

The result was that at forty-six thousand feet, seventy-three seconds into its mission, the *Challenger* disintegrated into several pieces. The Shuttle and its seven-member crew were lost. While findings were inconclusive as to the cause of death of the astronauts, whether they survived the initial breakup seemed inconsequential to Florida schoolchildren who witnessed the explosion, a country that saw the explosion on television many times and NASA employees who lost friends and colleagues. The country was stunned and numb from what it had witnessed.

Salvage operations commenced to locate as much of the destroyed Shuttle as possible. NASA, navy, air force and private contractors scoured the debris field. Priority was given to finding the crew compartment and retrieving any human remains. During the five-week period of March 7 through April 15, human remains, accounting for all seven crew members, were provided to the Armed Forces Institute of Pathology for examination and identification.

On April 29, the remains were taken from Kennedy Space Center to Dover Air Force Base. From there, the astronauts' remains were provided to the families for burial. Two members of the crew are interred at Arlington National Cemetery, one was cremated and the ashes scattered and the others are buried at cemeteries close to their homes.

As a result of the tragedy, Space Shuttle operations were immediately suspended and investigations commenced, primary among them the Rogers Commission, or the Presidential Commission on the Space Shuttle *Challenger* Accident. Led by William P. Rogers, the commission submitted a report critical of both NASA and Morton Thiokol Inc. for overlooking safety concerns regarding weather, O-rings and the solid rocket boosters. Multiple recommendations, including redesigning portions of the Shuttle and a restructuring of NASA management, were put forth. The commission was also critical of the increased launch schedule, stating that it created pressures to achieve unrealistic goals.

The *Challenger* tragedy led to a launch hiatus of almost three years. It would not be until September 29, 1988, that the next launch, *Discovery*, would occur. STS-26R would take a crew of five to space for a period of four days. In addition to regular experiments, the crew successfully launched a Tracking and Data Relay Satellite, part of a space communications system.

For fifteen years, the Shuttle program continued to operate safely, providing incredible amounts of data to scientists, assisting the mission of the International Space Station, servicing the Hubble Telescope and completing other important work. On January 16, 2003, *Columbia* launched as the 113th mission.

Seven crew members, including Ilan Ramon, the first Israeli astronaut, perished when *Columbia* disintegrated upon reentry into Earth's atmosphere after a flight of two weeks. It was determined that during liftoff, a piece of insulating foam broke away and struck thermal protection tiles on the exterior of the Shuttle, damaging the left wing. Video of the damage can be seen occurring eighty-two seconds after liftoff. The NASA-led Debris Assessment Team concluded after launch that there were no safety concerns from the foam impact, going so far as to tell the Shuttle crew that there was no reason for concern.

Upon reentry to Earth's atmosphere, hot air began to enter the damaged left wing and melt the structure. Sensors began sending danger alerts, but automatic controls made needed flight corrections. As the Shuttle continued its rapid descent over the western United States, pieces of debris could be seen falling from the craft. At 9:00 a.m., the craft began disintegrating over Texas. By 9:35 a.m., it was estimated that all debris from the explosion had reached the ground. There were no survivors.

The Columbia Accident Investigation Board concluded left wing damage from the foam impact to have been the most likely cause of the accident. NASA was faulted for not having given previous foam collisions thorough safety consideration. An overly ambitious flight schedule, often to assist the International Space Station, in the face of funding cuts was also deemed a cause.

The Shuttle program was again grounded, this time for another two years before *Discovery* took seven astronauts to space in July 2005. This mission marked a triumphant return to space for NASA, with the Shuttle completing a nearly two-week mission.

It would be another year before the next mission, with *Discovery* launching in July 2006. Missions began to become more frequent, but never again reaching the fevered pace of the early years. Missions were for longer periods, most averaging around two weeks. Many of these missions were geared toward the International Space Station. Supply replenishment, crew exchanges and ISS assembly became focal points of the Shuttle program.

In its investigation of the *Columbia* explosion, the investigation board declared that needed safety upgrades to the program were no longer cost efficient. Based on this finding and budgetary priorities, President George W. Bush announced in 2004 that the Shuttle program would come to an end once the International Space Station assembly was completed. A target date for 2010 was given. After thirty years, the Shuttle program would be permanently grounded.

There was still work to be completed, however. In 2009, shuttle astronauts made the last repairs to the Hubble Space Telescope. Later that year, the final shuttle landing at Edwards Air Force Base occurred. Always a favorite with the public, the final night launch of a shuttle occurred on April 5, 2010, when *Discovery* launched on a fifteen-day mission.

President Bush's 2010 goal was missed, and the Shuttle program continued in 2011. *Discovery* made its final launch on February 24, *Endeavour* launched on May 16 and *Atlantis* took the final shuttle crew to space, launching on July 8. When *Atlantis* landed at Kennedy Space Center on July 21, 2011, an era in space exploration truly ended.

Over thirty years, the Space Shuttle program flew 355 different individuals from sixteen countries more than 542 million miles. It deployed 180 payloads, including satellites. Repairs and construction were undertaken for multiple spacecraft, and more than two thousand experiments were performed. Despite the loss of fourteen astronauts on two missions, the program safely landed 133 flights.

During a successful three-decade span, NASA expanded its knowledge of space and other science, advanced safety standards both for space and everyday life and, perhaps most importantly, inspired a generation of dreamers who are continuing the goal of space travel today.

The Artemis program will be NASA's triumphant return to the Moon, more than fifty years after the first lunar landing. Planned for a 2025 launch, the *Artemis III* will take astronauts to the "lunar south pole" region, an area previously unexplored by man. This mission will be a partnership between NASA and SpaceX, which is developing the human landing system that *Artemis* will use.

Longer-range NASA plans include continued unmanned explorations to the planet Mars, with a goal of landing humans on the red planet. Many considerations will be involved in this, however, as technology, launch availability (a concern that is much more complicated than that of a Shuttle mission), cost, political willpower and astronaut safety will weigh heavily on any decisions regarding sending astronauts to another planet.

Space exploration and transportation are no longer the realm of governments only. Billionaires are now some of the primary drivers of space exploration. Three private companies are currently the leaders—Elon Musk and SpaceX are perhaps the most well known. Others include Blue Origin, headed by Jeff Bezos of Amazon, and Richard Branson and Virgin Galactic.

SpaceX launches are a common occurrence off the Florida coast, as its *Falcon* rockets can be seen taking payloads to space. The *Falcon* is a partly reusable system in which the rocket boosters are able to return safely to Earth and be reused, helping provide considerable cost savings. The *Falcon 9* is able to transport humans to and from the International Space Station while also launching communication satellites, often as part of the SpaceX-owned Starlink space-based internet service. Not content to be a delivery service, SpaceX has plans to send unmanned crews to Mars, with a longer-term goal of sending humans to the planet. Deep-space exploration is an even longer-term goal.

Blue Origin is owned by Amazon founder Jeff Bezos. Blue Origin is perhaps best known for celebrity launches, including Bezos himself and the then ninety-year-old William Shatner, Captain Kirk in the original *Star Trek* television series. Bezos and Blue Origin have an ambitious goal of creating Orbital Reef. According to the Blue Origin website, "Orbital Reef will be the premier mixed-use space station in low Earth orbit for commerce, research, and tourism by the end of this decade [2020s]."

This business park in the sky is planned to orbit about 250 miles above Earth's surface. Users will be able to lease space for uses such as research, manufacturing, exploration, advertising or to establish an address. Blue Origin hopes to make space travel a more attractive and affordable option for non-astronauts.

Virgin Galactic is the brainchild of Richard Branson, founder of the Virgin line of businesses. Virgin Galactic is designed to be a space experience venture, rather than having scientific or research goals. Virgin Galactic offers very short-duration flights, averaging less than fifteen minutes and reaching around fifty-five miles above Earth's surface. Currently, Virgin Galactic does not operate launches from Florida.

The aviation and aerospace industries are a crucial cog in the economic engine of the state of Florida. From a low of 79,000 jobs in 2004, the Florida Department of Economic Opportunity (FDEO) reports that for the year 2020, there were 2,568 businesses in the aviation and aerospace industries, employing 115,000 people. For the combined industries, this represented a drop from 2019 of under 4,000 jobs. During that one-year period, the aviation industry lost 5,500 jobs, while the aerospace industry added almost 1,600 positions. When examining these numbers, the impact of COVID-19 on the aviation and tourism industries must be considered. This pandemic severely hampered airlines, as business and leisure travel plans were modified or canceled. Decreased demand forced airlines to make labor reductions they might not otherwise have made. With the strong rebound in both domestic and international tourism, future reports should show a rebound in employment in the aviation sector.

Wages for those employed in the aviation and aerospace industries trend higher than the average Florida wage earner. In 2020, the average yearly wage in the aviation industry was around $71,500 and over $100,000 in the aerospace industry. In considering all industries, the FDEO reported an annual wage of just under $56,000 for the state. When the state, counties and cities put forth incentives for stable companies with well-paying jobs, they are often hoping to lure businesses from the aviation and aerospace industries.

Florida has played an outsized role in the race for space. With weather that is usually cooperative, Cape Canaveral and Kennedy Space Center have proven ideal for launching rockets, and humans, into space. From the earliest experiments of the *Bumper* program through the exciting opportunities being offered by SpaceX and others, Florida is a leader in the space industry. When a human eventually walks on the surface of Mars, it is highly likely they will have launched from Florida.

AFTERWORD

The problem with trying to document the history of aviation in Florida is a common problem for historians simply because the scope of the subject is so immense and because so much activity went unrecorded. To make the task of writing a history of aviation in the Sunshine State more difficult is the limitation of space mandated by the publisher. As a result, what the authors have done is provide a general background of the subject and create a basis for further investigation of the subject. In perusing the available literature on the subject, other historians have faced the same problem. The subject is vast, but slowly sources are emerging that add substance to questions and documentation for events. Recent scholarship from talented amateur historians on the evolution of local airports and the rise and fall of local airlines has helped to clarify and expand our knowledge of the aviation industry in Florida.

One thing is certain: whatever new technologies are developed and regardless of the complexities of implementing these technologies, the Sunshine State will emerge as a leader in the effort to take humans higher, faster and farther into the skies. The proliferation of space-oriented companies venturing into fields once dominated solely by government agencies is proof of that. The clear skies that beckoned early aviators to the Sunshine State still remain, although the once small population has grown to more than 22 million persons. The lure of the heavens and human ingenuity combine to make Florida a center for science, adventure and curiosity!

BIBLIOGRAPHY

Air Transport Association of America. "Air Transport Facts and Figures." Report.

Brown, Warren J. *Florida's Aviation History: The First One Hundred Years*. Largo, FL: Aero-Medical Consultants Inc., 1994.

Buker, George E. *Sun, Sand and Water: A History of the Jacksonville District of the Army Corps of Engineers, 1821–1975*. Washington, D.C.: Government Printing Office, n.d.

Colburn, David R. "Florida Politics in the Twentieth Century." In *The New History of Florida*. Edited by Michael Gannon. Gainesville: University Press of Florida, 1996.

Davis, Aurora E. "The Development of the Major Commercial Airlines in Dade County, Florida: 1945–1970." *Tequesta* 32 (1972).

Day, Dwayne A., John Logsdon and Brian Latell, eds. *Eye in the Sky: The Story of the CORONA Spy Satellites*. Washington, D.C.: Smithsonian Institution, 1998.

Daytona Beach News Journal. "$42,931 Project at Airport Gets Federal Okeh." July 22, 1935.

Faherty, William Barnaby. *Florida's Space Coast: The Impact of NASA on the Sunshine State*. Gainesville: University Press of Florida, 2002.

Florida Department of Economic Opportunity, Bureau of Workforce Statistics and Economic Research. *Labor Market Industry Profile: Florida Aviation & Aerospace Industry*. Tallahassee, FL, 2021.

Florida Historical Quarterly: Special Issue, Celebrating the 50th Anniversary of NASA in Florida (1958–2008) 87, no. 2 (Fall 2008).

Fuller, Walter P. "'Early Birds' of Florida." *Florida Historical Quarterly* 38, no. 1 (July 1959): 63–66.

Hausman, William J. "Juan Terry Trippe (1899–1981)." In *Encyclopedia of History of American Management.* Edited by Morgen Witzel. London: Bloomsbury Publishing, PLC, 2005.

Henderson, David P. *Sunshine Skies: Historic Commuter Airlines of Florida & Georgia*. N.p.: Zeus Press, 2008.

Higham, Robin. "Air Power in World War I, 1914–1918." In *War in the Air, 1914–1918.* Edited by Alan Stephens. Fairbairn: Royal Australian Air Force, Aerospace Centre, 1994.

Johnson, Edward C. *Marine Corps Aviation: The Early Years, 1912–1940.* Washington, D.C.: Headquarters, U.S. Marine Corps, History and Museums Division, 1991.

Kerstein, Robert. *Politics and Growth in Twentieth Century Tampa*. Gainesville: University Press of Florida, 2001.

Knetsch, Joe, and Pamela Gibson. *Florida in World War I.* Charleston, SC: The History Press, 2021.

Knetsch, Joe, Nick Wynne and Robert Redd. *Florida at Sea: A Maritime History*. Charleston, SC: The History Press, 2023.

Knowlton, Christopher. *Bubble in the Sun: The Florida Boom of the 1920s and How It Brought on the Great Depression*. New York: Simon & Schuster, 2020.

McCarthy, Kevin M. *Aviation in Florida*. Sarasota, FL: Pineapple Press, 2003.

McColister, John, and Diann Davis. *The Sky Is Home: The Story of Embry-Riddle—The World's Leading Aviation/Aerospace University*. Middle Village, NY: Jonathan David Publishers, 1996.

McGuire, Raymond G. "Chapman Field—The Evolution of a South Dade Army Airdrome." United States Department of Agriculture. https://www.ars.usda.gov/southeast-area/miami-fl/subtropical-horticulture-research/docs/chapman-field-the-evolution-of-a-south-dade-army-airdrome.

Miami-Dade Aviation Department. "History of Miami International Airport." https://www.miami-airport.com/library/pdfdoc/MIA%20History%20Book%202020%20small.pdf.

Mormino, Gary R. *Land of Sunshine, Land of Dreams*. Gainesville: University Press of Florida, 2005.

National Aeronautics and Space Administration. "The Apollo Program." https://www.nasa.gov/the-apollo-program.

———. "Bumper: The Story Behind the First Launches from the Cape." https://www.nasa.gov/missions/highlights/webcasts/history/bumper-qa.html.

Orbital Reef. https://www.orbitalreef.com.

Potter, William C., et al. *Melbourne Orlando International Airport: A History from 1928 to 2022*. N.p.: independently published, 2022.

Provenzo, Eugene, Jr. "St. Petersburg-Tampa Airboat Line." *Florida Historical Quarterly* 58, no. 1 (July 1979): 72–77.

Raines, Edgar F., Jr. *Eyes of the Artillery: The Origins of Modern U. S. Army Aviation in World War II*. Washington, D.C.: Center of Military History, 2000.

Reilly, Thomas. "The Birth of National Airlines: The St. Petersburg Years, 1934–1939." *Tampa Bay History* 19, no. 1 (June 1997).

Richards, Rose Connett. "Coffee, Tea or Milk—the Early Years." *Historical Association of Southern Florida Update* 15, no. 4 (November 1988): 9–12.

Rinehart, Kathryn. "Naval Aviation in Florida." Florida in World War I, 2017. https://floridawwi.cah.ucf.edu/?p=342.

Serling, Robert J. *From the Captain to the Colonel: An Informal History of Eastern Airlines*. New York: Dial Press, 1980.

Shell-Weiss, Melanie. *Coming to Miami: A Social History*. Gainesville: University Press of Florida, 2009.

Stronge, William B. *The Sunshine Economy: An Economic History of Florida Since the Civil War*. Gainesville: University Press of Florida, 2008.

Time. "Aeronautics: Merchant Aerial." https://content.time.com/time/subscriber/article/0,33009,753876,00.html.

Wynne, Nick. *Tin Can Tourists in Florida: 1900–1970*. Charleston, SC: Arcadia Publishing, 1999.

Wynne, Nick, and Joe Knetsch, eds. *Edge of Armageddon: Florida and the Cuban Missile Crisis*. Denver, CO: Outskirts Press, 2018.

Wynne, Nick, and Joseph Knetsch. *Florida in the Great Depression: Desperation and Defiance*. Charleston, SC: The History Press, 2012.

Wynne, Nick, and Richard Moorhead. *Florida in World War II: Floating Fortress*. Charleston, SC: The History Press, 2010.

———. *Paradise for Sale: Florida's Booms and Busts*. Charleston, SC: The History Press, 2010.

ABOUT THE AUTHORS

NICK WYNNE is the Emeritus Executive Director of the Florida Historical Society and a prolific author of fact and fiction. He lives with his wife, Debra, in a historic home in Rockledge, Florida. JOE KNETSCH is a graduate of Florida State University and the author of multiple books on Florida history. He retired from the Florida Department of Natural Resources and now serves as an expert witness in court cases involving land usage and navigable water rights. He is a much-in-demand speaker for various historical groups. ROBERT J. REDD is a native Floridian with a longtime interest in history. He holds degrees from Stetson University and American Public University. He is a member of the Florida Historical Society, Southern Historical Society, American Battlefield Trust and other organizations. He is honored to be a part of this team in telling the story of Florida's aerial history.